Acclaim for
Lesbians in Committed Relationships

"Reading *Lesbians in Committed Relationships* is like listening to ordinary stories told by ordinary women, as we sit at the kitchen table with a cup of tea on a frosty morning or huddle around a warm fire in the blustery evening, hearing the stories in an extraordinary way. The sounds cascade over us in a rhythm of care and concern. And as often happens, the notes written in the margin shed light on what resides in the center. All couples and all women can learn from these narratives about relationship and community, about negotiating and compromise, about love and sharing, and about overcoming obstacles. We leave their presence feeling nurtured and somehow calmed."

—Victoria C. Dickerson, PhD, Clinical Psychologist,
Narrative Therapist, and Consultant, Aptos, CA

"Although I have never met the authors, I consider them my friends and comrades for putting into writing what the gay and lesbian communities have needed: role models for building satisfying relationships as truly decent and moral people in today's society. These role models share the stories of their intimate relationships throughout the book. They share their stories proudly and demonstrate that in any human relationship, regardless of sexual orientation, with pain comes happiness. In the end, love of friends and family are all you have; material possessions are temporary. I highly recommend this book for anyone who craves a sustaining and satisfying relationship."

—Terry White, Leader, Alternative Lives/Happy Families:
A Support Group for Gay and Lesbian Parents, Atwater, Ohio

"This is an extraordinary book with extraordinary stories. At the same time it describes ordinary people living ordinary lives. The narratives of this book are moving, they are fascinating, and they are growth-provoking for me and will be for the reader as well.

The book enables the counselor or therapist to enter the world of lesbian couples and their families. It is a privilege to learn from real people who live real lives. Every helping professional needs this book on the shelf, both for professional understanding and for helping parents and friends of lesbian couples to understand. Moreover, the book will be insightful and helpful to many lesbian couples as well."

—Allen E. Ivey, EdD, ABPP, Distinguished University
Professor (Emeritus), University of Massachusetts, Amherst

NOTES FOR PROFESSIONAL LIBRARIANS
AND LIBRARY USERS

This is an original book title published by Alice Street Editions, Harrington Park Press®, an imprint of The Haworth Press, Inc. Unless otherwise noted in specific chapters with attribution, materials in this book have not been previously published elsewhere in any format or language.

CONSERVATION AND PRESERVATION NOTES

All books published by The Haworth Press, Inc. and its imprints are printed on certified pH neutral, acid free book grade paper. This paper meets the minimum requirements of American National Standard for Information Sciences-Permanence of Paper for Printed Material, ANSI Z39.48-1984.

Lesbians in Committed Relationships

Extraordinary Couples, Ordinary Lives

ALICE STREET EDITIONS
Judith P. Stelboum
Editor in Chief

Lesbians in Committed Relationships
Extraordinary Couples, Ordinary Lives

Lynn Haley-Banez, PhD
Joanne Garrett

Alice Street Editions
Harrington Park Press®
An Imprint of The Haworth Press, Inc.
New York • London • Oxford

Published by

Alice Street Editions, Harrington Park Press®, an imprint of The Haworth Press, Inc., 10 Alice Street, Binghamton, NY 13904-1580.

Cover design by Lora Wiggins.

Library of Congress Cataloging-in-Publication Data

Haley-Banez, Lynn.
    Lesbians in committed relationships : extraordinary couples, ordinary lives / Lynn Haley-Banez, Joanne Garrett.
        p. cm.
Includes bibliographical references.
        ISBN 1-56023-208-0 (alk. paper)—ISBN 1-56023-209-9 (soft)
    1. Lesbians—United States—Case studies. 2. Gay couples—United States—Case studies. 3. Commitment (Psychology)—Case studies. I. Garrett, Joanne. II. Title.
HQ75.6.U5 H35 2002
305.48'9664—dc21
                                                                                                2002068759

I dedicate this to the four couples: Jill and Marge, Chris and Sarah, Rita and Sandy, and Lisa and Elaine; to my daughter Jordain; my life partner Arianne, with whom I continue to co-construct our story as a couple; my mother Marilyn King for her support of who I am; and Andrea and Wendy.

Lynn

For Mom and Dad, with love

Joanne

CONTENTS

Editor's Foreword

Alice Street Editions provides a voice for established as well as up-and-coming lesbian writers, reflecting the diversity of lesbian interests, ethnicities, ages, and class. This cutting-edge series of novels, memoirs, and nonfiction writing welcomes the opportunity to present controversial views, explore multicultural ideas, encourage debate, and inspire creativity from a variety of lesbian perspectives. Through enlightening, illuminating, and provocative writing, Alice Street Editions can make a significant contribution to the visibility and accessibility of lesbian writing and bring lesbian-focused writing to a wider audience. Recognizing our own desires and ideas in print is life sustaining, acknowledging the reality of who we are, as well as our place in the world, individually and collectively.

Judith P. Stelboum
Editor in Chief
Alice Street Editions

Acknowledgments

I would like to acknowledge my mentors, Dr. Linda Rogers and Dr. Beth Blue Swadener for encouraging me to follow my heart in working on this valuable project, and my co-author, Joanne Garrett, without whom this book would not exist. It is our shared dream and her courage, focus, and determination that turned a dream into a reality.

Lynn Haley-Banez, PhD

A wink and a nod to everyone who believes in me.

Joanne Garrett

NOTE

Some of the couples chose to use pseudonyms. Also, the names of many of the peripheral characters have been changed for reasons of privacy.

Many extraneous words, such as *uh, um, like,* and *you know,* have been removed from the conversations to make reading easier. Otherwise, none of the conversations have been altered.

Introduction

Everyone has a story.

And everyone loves to have an audience.

We tell our stories to reveal where we come from, what we think and believe, where we want to go. We describe our selves, silently to ourselves, on paper in our journals and pictures, aloud to our friends and acquaintances, in actions to the world. Our stories can be seen in the way we carry ourselves, the people in our lives, our creativity and recreations, in our smiling embraces and our shyly downturned eyes.

Our stories define us. They show where we have been and how that has had an influence; they carry those people who have made impressions on our hearts and minds; they can be told in broad outline, in minute detail.

Our stories cannot confine us. Every moment, each encounter can influence our stories. We might meet someone and follow that same path for a while; we might bounce off the briefest of meetings and find a new direction. One person might become our touchstone for spirituality, another the reason we know how to change the oil in our cars. We might find ourselves leading others to our paths; we could be teachers, mentors, guides.

All the people, places, and things we encounter in our lives are parts of our story. And our stories are not static. Just as we continue to live and grow, we can select, edit, and construct the stories of our lives, to decide how we present ourselves to the world.

There are all sorts of layers to our stories and all sorts of degrees to which we reveal ourselves. We might let our most intimate friends and family members see and hear all of our stories. We might limit the stories by which the rest of the world knows us—our personal stories might not translate well in the workplace. Some stories might not be told to anyone except ourselves as we lie in the dark and think, wonder, dream, even dream harder.

We want to know and be known. That is a factor in the meaning of our stories. To be heard gives us certainty that we are alive, human, a member of a community. It is that drive, that yearning for knowledge, that brings us to this subject.

Lesbians who are in long-term relationships are, to a large extent, unknown. This is partly because they are not allowed to tell their stories. Whether it is because of the extent to which they are out, the political and cultural climates in which they live, their hesitation to speak, or just a lack of caring on the part of others, their stories—the very definition of their existence—are not always welcomed, accepted, heard.

These women are storehouses of information, knowledge, and experience. Their words give us a history, not only of one person, but a group, a community that continues to evolve. This history in turn provides a foundation for understanding where we are today, where we might want to go. Their passions fuel the fires of their relationships. They share values and beliefs and dreams; they have memories of the actions, mistakes, and triumphs of the past; and they are seers of visions that shape and define the future. They can shape hope. And now, they are willing to share these stories and all that they carry on their journeys.

Lesbians create private and public stories—narratives—of their relationships despite their invisibility to society and the absence of social support and legitimization in a heterocentrist culture. This leaves lesbians to define the rules. By doing so, they can tap into great freedom and endless choices. Because they are often outcasts of society, family, and/or the workplace, lesbians display remarkable courage and dip into wellsprings of creativity to live and love. What better way to develop role models for ourselves, to show all that there is hope and a bright future, than by allowing these women to tell their stories? The compelling nature of these narratives and the relative lack of exposure they have had led to the development of this project. It is time to expand on previous studies and build on those foundations. It is time to share our stories.

Interesting? What could be more interesting than the histories, hopes, and fears of women who have been in committed relationships for more than ten years? These relationships, not acknowledged, not sanctioned, hardly seen, and not supported by society, do not exist in a vacuum. Somehow, these women have built and sustained these relationships and they are ready to tell about their experiences. As a result, we can see how their stories as a couple developed, how the growth and deepening of the stories paralleled the growth and deepening of the relationship, and how events and words have influenced their stories and thus their relationship.

The term "narrative" is used in the broadest sense of a story, that which has a beginning, middle, and end. What we have with these four couples are definite beginnings and middles. However, there are no endings to these narratives, because they are still developing and thriving. These stories are still being written.

This book was written for couples so they might have role models, and so they can see that long-term, monogamous, intimate relationships do exist. The truth is there. If they understand the dynamics of a couple's narrative, they can seek ways to create healthier stories. They can determine influences—positive and negative—and decide what impact these influences will have on their own narratives. The couples whose stories appear in these pages can show various ways to create and live a story.

This book is for individuals, so they can see that long-term relationships can work, and discover some tools that might help.

This book is for counselors. If they can understand the creation of a couple's narrative and the influences on it, they will be able to help that couple enhance their relationship by assisting a rewrite of the narrative. They can help identify the influences and keep the couple on the path of a healthy relationship.

This book is for anyone who has, or wants to have, hope. If we understand how stories are created, built, and influenced, we can use that knowledge to rewrite and edit stories for healthier relationships in our own lives.

Come along. Listen.

How did it come about that these eight women found an outlet for their stories? Why are these four couples the focus?

In light of the political, religious and cultural atmospheres in this nation and the variations that appear from region to region, is it any wonder that lesbian couples in long-term, committed, monogamous relationships might be close to invisible? And that some prefer it that way?

These women are diverse in race, socioeconomic level, age, and education. They are women in same-gender couples; they are monogamous and committed; they have been together for at least ten years; as it turns out, they all live in the same geographic region. Of course, they are willing to participate and share their lives.

The women were invited to fill out a questionnaire about demographics before the first interview, which covered fifteen open-ended questions. A second interview was held, to correct transcripts and to follow up with two more questions on subjects that came up during the first interviews with all four couples. The couples also chose photographs and/or scrapbooks for a visual history and asked a member of the family or friend to be interviewed about the couple. They were asked to share a holiday, ritual, or ceremony that held meaning for them. And it was suggested that they might want to keep a journal during the study.

Some of the couples were able to participate fully; others, because of time constraints, travel, or other scheduling problems, participated in the majority of interviews but not all. Some chose to use pseudonyms.

Finally, after a few years, another visit allows a catch-up.

JILL AND MARGE

It is cold and snowy—just another February day in this Midwest town, which the Chamber of Commerce likes to call a recovering rust-belt town. Jill and Marge appear with baby in tow—Jill is forty-two, Marge is thirty-six, and Elizabeth is ten months—and head into the family room. A fire has been laid and it casts its colors into the room. There is freshly brewed coffee and fixings on a table and plenty of comfortable places to sit.

The baby stays with her moms during the interviews and the moms take turns cuddling, comforting, and holding the baby, changing diapers, and meeting other needs. The tiny girl, clearly not willing to miss anything, simply won't go down for a nap.

Jill and Marge have been together—in a monogamous relationship— for twelve years; they met through friends, and four months later, began living together. Jill has a master's degree and Marge has a bachelor's, and they describe themselves as middle-middle class (Marge was raised in an upper-class household, while Jill was raised in a middle-middle class home; both are of white European-American descent). They are under a bit more stress than usual—one is starting a new job and they are raising their girl—which reminds them that what time they have for one another is sacred.

The second interview takes place in April, a rainy and cold day, casting a gray pallor on the predominantly working-class neighborhood. Yet, it is so easy to warm up with chatter about babies and how they grow; their daughter, now nearly a year old, plays with her toys.

The women have told some members of their families and some friends about their relationship, forming their inner circle. They move in a social circle that includes heterosexual and gay friends and family of choice. They see themselves as "white, middle-class women struggling to pay the bills." It is not hard to see how tired they can get, but they rarely lose patience with one another, nor with the baby. They share affectionate glances and coo with their girl, who is clearly a most important aspect of their lives. They speak to the baby matter-of-factly in conversational tones, answer screeches, repay smiles, and receive head-butts of affection.

Both women are aware that they are not "like the people next door," says Jill, and believe that any strangers who see them together would assume they are just friends. They describe themselves as "caring people, down to earth, a good sense of humor, trying to make the world a better place," says Jill, and Marge adds: "Just regular working people. Trying to be kind to others, make things easy for others. Just an average couple with a mortgage and bills." They prefer to keep most of their displays of affection private.

CHRIS AND SARAH

Mom, apple pie, and baseball . . . Chris and Sarah live in a rural area in Ohio, not far from the Amish communities. They own and operate a bed and breakfast, and during the week, Chris lives and works in a major city.

Dogs greet all arrivals at the bed and breakfast on this afternoon. A young woman doing yard work directs visitors to the lobby. Chris and Sarah are with some weekend guests, and introduce them, along with Jane, a long-time friend whom Chris and Sarah consider family. In their private home, a separate building on the property, a comfortable couch, a rocking chair, and a coffee table are arranged to allow perfect viewing angles of the television. Their favorite baseball team is playing and Chris and Sarah like to occasionally check the score.

They have been in a monogamous relationship for eighteen-plus years. Sarah, an African-American woman from a poor/working-class background, is in her early sixties, and Chris, who has a white European background, is in her early fifties.

Both women find comfort and grace in the earth. Just as easily as welcoming friends for a ball game, they invite friends to walk the land and enjoy the warm, sunny spring day. Sarah has a particular affinity for a garden in the shape of a medicine wheel. She has developed the plot, which is soothing and rejuvenating. Sarah is often described as "being." Chris, who is nearing retirement, often knits—as much to keep her hands busy as to create wearable art—and is thought of as a "doer." Friends say they tease her because she always wants to stay in conversations but also wants to be busy and productive. Taking up knitting has given her a way to do both. She and Sarah look forward to those retirement days of quiet leisure, or at least as much as they might find while running a bed and breakfast.

It is the very connection of these individual souls that allows Chris and Sarah to focus on the women's community, especially the lesbian community. They display their affection for one another privately and draw strength and solace from that private relationship. They clearly are so comfortable in their relationship that they are able to give much energy to the community. A women's weekend in late May sees dozens of women gather to help with planting and weeding, building and repairing. And they remain mindful of building their community.

They also have taken in a child. Sarah's niece had a child fifteen years ago and for all that time, she and her son have been part of the household. He has slowly wrapped his great aunts around his little finger, and they have the photos and the happy memories to prove it.

RITA AND SANDY

These women have built their family by choice—they have been in a monogamous relationship for thirteen years—and have told only some siblings and their most trusted friends that they are a couple. A sibling says that family members mostly know about the relationship, yet it is rarely a topic for discussion.

And, it is family that is a pivotal focus in their lives. They have tales and photos and fond memories of their adventures with nieces and nephews and outings with friends, whom they have welcomed into their family. There are visits to the zoo, scavenger hunts in the backyard, occasional trips to New York City for a show.

This welcoming nature is reflected by the hugs they give visitors and the comfort of their home, which is in Ohio in a rural area not far from a working-class town. Sandy, a softball player, is in her early forties, while Rita, a softball fan, is in her late thirties. They were raised in working-class families and describe their lives as upper-middle class. Rita and Sandy are white.

On a bitterly cold day in February, everyone dresses in layers and hovers close to the fireplace, which glows with warmth and keeps the dog lying quietly nearby. In May, a screened-in porch becomes a chamber for the bird orchestra and a viewing area for the buds, shoots, and blooms of the season.

Rita and Sandy enjoy joking with one another and occasionally touch one another affectionately on the arm or leg. There are times when they look each other in the eyes and "they think no one else in the world is living," Sandy's sister says, adding, "When you're around them, too, you get the sense . . . they know what each other's thinking."

Sandy has earned a medical degree, and Rita holds a master's degree. They met, started dating and, in about a year, began living together.

They have a getaway spot—a cabin on a lake. They like to take friends and family there for cookouts, boating, relaxing, and recharging. Both meditate alone, and on weekends, they meditate together. They try to maintain a vegetarian diet, even vegan. They love to bicycle together.

LISA AND ELAINE

A lump in Elaine's breast has been one of the major tests for this couple. They have been in a committed, monogamous relationship for twelve years.

These women display an "intensity, commitment, trust, respect, passion, and fierce commitment to work on their relationship," a friend, Bridget, says. It is that strength that pulls them through health crises, as well as the glare of publicity because one is in public office.

They are both in their forties and they live in a moderately populated, blue-collar town that gives them easy access to their sailboat. They describe themselves as upper class. Lisa says she is of white English descent and Elaine describes herself as white, German, and Irish. Both say they come from blue-collar families. Both hold postgraduate degrees.

Lisa and Elaine are out to many people, but not everyone. Because of the nature of their jobs, they must be selective, and they tend to socialize predominantly with heterosexual couples. Yet, this has done little to discourage the passionate nature of their relationship. They share affectionate glances, touch one another on the arm or leg, give foot rubs. And, they use humor as a balance in their relationship.

This couple has turned out to be a role model for their friend, Bridget, who says: "I have learned so much about what it takes to make a relationship work and to endure."

Another test of this relationship was the first run for public office, during which Lisa was not out to the public, and always made her campaign appearances with a gay man as a stand-in partner.

Where do they find peace and quiet with one another? They find it in their bright, light kitchen, with their dog subtly on standby for dropped crumbs, and on their sailboat. One partner is a member of a yacht club, but given the political and social climate of the area, the other must sign in as a guest. Still, they board their sailboat and go to where none of that can reach them, to a place where they can reach one another during precious private time. Sailing and boating have been a part of their life together, with the breadth of their maritime skills growing with the size of their boats. It is on the water—salt or fresh, day or night, far from home or at the dock of the yacht club—that they replenish themselves.

It's the Story . . .

When we tell of ourselves, put our stories on paper, turn our tales to text, we discover several common themes. And these themes come under the umbrella of healthy relationships.

Among the common threads running through our couples' stories are questions about the sane division of labor, examples of how to be in a relationship and how to be in the world.

Each of our couples has figured out who will handle which chores to keep the household running. Who will take out the garbage, fill the water bowl for the cats, clean up after dinner, pick up the dry cleaning, set the VCR, return calls from friends with invitations to dinner? Who will have the time to return books to the library, stop at the grocery store, think about dinner? Who will work late because this is prime time for overtime and the budget sure could use it? Who will plan the getaway, the vacation that will allow both to reclaim their well-rested and recharged selves? All of this is negotiated, sometimes on a day-to-day basis.

Each of these women entered a relationship determined not to follow the example of parents. All the women express some degree of dismay that they see their parents' relationships as unhealthy, and they agree that they work on what they define as a healthy relationship. Each of these couples has learned to function in a society that does not always accept, and hardly celebrates, a same-gender relationship.

These themes all are based on an egalitarian relationship—one constructed by the couple. The qualities of their relationships form the foundation on which they build their daily lives. Those foundations? Just as one would suspect, the qualities that provide strength and resilience to the relationship: trust, integrity, sensitivity, shared interests, mutual respect, caring, compassion, a willingness to work on the relationship, and a willingness to compromise.

This is reflected by Jill and Marge, when they are asked to describe their relationship and how they might be seen by an outsider.

JILL: I would say, oh, caring people, down to earth, a good sense of humor, trying to make the world a better place . . .

MARGE: Respect. What's that song? R-E-S-P . . . I mean, we have the more normal family-type relationship and trust and caring that most of her friends don't seem to have.

J: I think that they would see us helping each other and we both take an equal responsibility for the baby and . . . you know, it's not like one is more dominant than the other or more responsibility is placed on the other person.

The collaborative nature of their decisions is summed up by Jill: "I feel like we work as a team. Just the other day we were saying that we need to set new goals, like we set goals as a team. . . . We set a goal to buy a house and then have a baby, and, so all that kind of stuff has been accomplished and now we're looking at where we're going to go from here. So, it's mutual decision-making."

Ask Sandy and Rita how their story as a couple has evolved and it is clear what qualities they believe are necessary for a beginning. They discuss their commitment to working on their relationship and the importance of shared interests:

RITA: OK. Trusting. I might even say that Sandy and I have a very satisfying, monogamous relationship of almost thirteen years, and that I have a very loving partner and that I've been blessed. That I'm committed to improving myself and growing first and . . . probably the second-most important thing is my relationship with my partner and my commitment to her and that I would do just about anything, I would work on just about anything. I will continue to be in therapy if I have to, so that I can continue to grow and so that our relationship could be the very best that it can be.

SANDY: I've been in a couple of other long-term relationships that it didn't seem like we worked on the relationship. It seemed like we thought it should just be and have a life of its own and we didn't have to work on it, but, I don't know if it's because I'm older or wiser or what, but I know that that doesn't work all the time and that if we wanted our relationship to grow, we would have to commit to it and really have to work on it, and I love Rita very much and I do want us to stay together, so that's what I'm doing, I'll say, working on our relationship. And, even though it's like working, you know, it's definitely worth it and it's fun and we have a lot of common interests and we do have a good time, we have fun together. We do a lot of things together.

R: Enjoying each other's company and wanting to do things together and a lot of, all kinds of activities that we do together. We take walks together, we plan vacations together, we look forward to planning vacations together and spending time together. [She laughs as she defines that time as "not around here and work, you know."]

Just as any story can incorporate the past and build on it, it is clear these women bring their experiences into their relationships. It is even more clear that, in the beginning, they were alert to their pasts, looking for mistakes or missteps they might have made and seeking ways to avoid pitfalls in their new relationships, all the while keeping the basic themes running through their stories.

Each couple describes the relationship in terms of a headline, the title of a book, or a song. Chris almost immediately has a defining phrase for her time with Sarah.

CHRIS: We made it past nine years. Since we both were in relationships before that were nine years long. So we were, both of us wanted to give ourselves a good bit after nine years to where we were really able to sort of celebrate our relationship. We had sort of a celebration and we've been together twelve years. And nine years was for us rather pivotal.

Sarah points out that they each had learned some hard lessons in past relationships, one of which was giving up their individuality and becoming enmeshed with her partner. Both were acutely aware of the ramifications of such action and both were acutely aware of trying to avoid that.

SARAH: I think we consciously went into this relationship knowing that's how it would be. And I don't see destructive, hard, . . . as the other relationships that we both were in, that we gave up who we were and we consciously said that we would never ask the other person to do that or allow ourselves to do that.

They defined for themselves the difference between losing one's self to a relationship and being dependent on a partner. They learned they could lean on one another and remain individual; they came to be secure in their sense of true and honest partnership. Each brings particular skills and beliefs and feelings to the partnership, each equally important. Among the basics that have made this partnership possible are mutual respect, caring, and compassion. Without those building blocks, their individuality could not survive, much less thrive.

And, because of the strength of their partnership, they have been able to expand their story to include another relationship—that of community.

It is another chapter in their story as a couple, and an important area of work for them, definitely a shared interest. They can branch out in their relationship because of the strength of their relationship.

SARAH: Community is probably the primary goal in life.

CHRIS: And for some wonderful reason, there's just, there's no jealousy that exists in our relationship. So, we, both of us, can have terrific relationships outside with other couples, with other individuals as couples. But as individuals to individuals. It has nothing to do with how we feel about each other or how we deal with our relationship.

What better example of compassion than to build community? What better way to welcome others into their lives than to invite them to stay on the land, to visit the bed and breakfast, to participate in a work weekend?

Other than the first six months of their relationship, Chris and Sarah have not lived together full time. During the week, Chris is in the city, working. Enter, the community. Calling Jane a friend would be a disservice to the depth and power of their relationship. Jane, simply, is a member of the family, and the first woman to be part of their community. And, they continue to add women, build their community, and follow their hearts in these relationships.

It is the community and their commitment to the land that serves as a metaphor for Sarah and Chris's model of a relationship.

SARAH: Like we do not believe in the concept of . . . we're a throw-away society. We believe in the concept that you recycle and you reuse. And, we try not to do things that are wasteful or things that will deliberately hurt other people.

CHRIS: You know, that's sort of true in terms of relationships, too. We really try as much as we can with relationships with people not to, when there's problems, to not just throw it away.

IT ISN'T OZZIE AND HARRIET

Each woman is willing to tell her story of growing up and watching her parents in their relationships. And each woman has decided she wants something different, a new path, a direction not yet explored. The women have notions of what a healthy relationship might be; these notions are based on conscious attempts to "not be like" their parents' relationships, which they describe as unhealthy.

Rita and Sandy discuss this at length. Rita speaks of her family and how family members influence her couple's story with Sandy.

RITA: The other thing is . . . the role model that I had for a couple. My parents, growing up was, in my opinion, awful. You know, my parents are alcoholics, my father is a very authoritative kind of person, and, I mean, conversation didn't exist. I mean, you were told what to do and how to do it and there was my mother, the victim, so you get the persecutor-victim role thing going on and that's what I saw my whole life.

I knew that that's not what I wanted and, you know, I really wanted it to be more of a loving thing where we each wanted to spend time together and talk with each other.

SANDY: And in an equal relationship. Not controlled. Not one person being more controlling than the other and, so we've really had to work on balance, too.

Many of the women speak of how this could be uncharted territory—if they grew up watching their role models and didn't like those stories, they could choose to change it for themselves. Yet, where would they find a suitable pattern that would incorporate the qualities they believe are important?

Some women turn to counselors and explore such questions. Some have stopped therapy, some seek intermittent counseling, some see therapists regularly. But one of the reasons for seeking counseling is shared: To find the way to build a healthy relationship. When Jill and Marge speak of their parents, they tell of the method they choose.

JILL: I just never wanted to be like my parents. So, I was going to do everything opposite that they did. Or just to be respectful of people . . . which was the opposite of my parents. But there was no single person that I'm trying to be like.

MARGE: That's basically how I've been.

Chris and Sarah have their parents as examples. However, they both have chosen and developed extended families, the roots not only for their growing community but also for ideas about healthy relationships.

CHRIS: I think a healthy relationship, there has to be, no matter if people feel comfortable with it, like it, don't like it, whatever, there has to be communication. Because, if you don't communicate, you're always going to have an unhealthy relationship. You can't read each other's minds.

And, communication's not easy for either one of us and especially not for me and I've had to work at it a lot. And I think a lot of other stuff, if you have a similar set of values, I think that the relationship probably isn't even going to be really healthy if you don't have a similar set of values, things you believe in. I think that's real important. You know, if I didn't think it was important, that trust wasn't important and she did, it's not going to work.

And, they explore where these ideas might have come from.

SARAH: And where did I learn it? I don't know. Maybe I've always known it. . . . Maybe it's one of those lessons that I learned in another life.

CHRIS: It certainly was around, unhealthy enough. I grew up with it. . . . We did some work on making it healthy and with a group and individual therapy.

S: And, also I think that there's been a part about us that knows what's good for us. We learned to listen to ourselves. To think we're important.

Chris speaks of two women who arrive as guests at the bed and breakfast. They talk about relationships for a few hours and Chris and Sarah both find the conversation to be fascinating and enlightening.

CHRIS: It was a great, it was a fantastic discussion.

SARAH: And so we'll never be the same tomorrow.

These women are acutely aware of their growth, individually and as a couple. But, where to look for role models, for living examples of healthy relationships? So many lesbian couples remain invisible, it is difficult to find older couples for role models. The couples of today might very well be pioneers—without role models and growing into that role for others.

Rita repeats to Sandy that she wants to look into the future of their relationship, and she knows what sort of crystal ball will provide that vision.

RITA: I have said to friends that what would be really neat for me would be to meet a couple that's maybe sixty or seventy or eighty that have been together thirty-five, forty years, and that have been very committed to each, well, I want to be them.

> They've gone through it, they have been really committed to each other, to their own health, you know, to professional help if they've needed that . . .

> Just to hear their stories and kind of like a mentor or role model . . . for me . . . for the next thirty-five, forty years. I just think that would be really neat personally to meet women like that and I don't know of any couples.

DIVIDE AND CONQUER

Another major theme of the couples' narratives is negotiating the roles each fills. Who does what, day-to-day, to keep the household running, and how do the partners decide?

ELAINE: We just kind of figured out what we did according to our talents and wants and all of that. But part of the problem was that during that first four months, she saw me doing all that stuff and kind of said, "Well, Elaine must be the one that's going to do all this stuff in this relationship."

That gets a laugh from both Elaine and Lisa.

ELAINE: And, I'm going, "Where is she, why isn't she picking up the ball here?" So, I think what I brought was a real sense of egalitarian. We're both in this, we're both responsible. And you brought in a much more traditional role, you know, where one person is the designated house person, takes care of those kinds of things.

It seems that things have fallen into place a bit more quickly for Sandy and Rita. They gravitate toward the chores they enjoy, have skill for, have the time to do. Self-determination works best for them.

SANDY: I thought that we talked about it, didn't we?

RITA: Not much.

S: Not like sat down and talked about . . .

R: No.

S: It just kind of happened.

R: It happened because you're real handy. You're like more of what you would consider the male role.

S: Mmmm.

R: You know, and I'm more of the female role in traditional society. You can fix anything. I'm not mechanical, you're mechanical. I don't have an interest in electricity and plumbing.

Marge and Jill try to take equal responsibility for the chores and responsibilities, but don't have a set way of negotiating who does what. They also are acutely aware of what roles society might presume for each partner.

MARGE: I guess that we don't have stereotypical roles as a husband and wife. You know, we're just more like friends that would help each other out. Although I do take the garbage out, so that's . . . I guess we just started doing it. I just did it.

JILL: Yeah, and I bring the garbage cans back in. You know, she takes them out, the garbage people dump them off, and the next day, I bring them in.

I guess people would see it as being more equal, more of a partnership than like stereotypical, well, this person has the financial responsibility and then this person stays home and takes care of the baby.

Like our neighbors are a heterosexual couple. She stays home with the two kids. He leaves probably at six, if not earlier, in the morning and comes home after seven at night. And he's in bed by ten. He sees the kids for a little bit but he doesn't help at all. So, she's got the responsibility of the two kids plus all that other stuff.

You know, then if the leaves need raked, then you're outside, then pick up the rake. But the stuff that we do do, like Marge mows the lawn, only because Marge likes to mow the lawn and I don't care about mowing it.

Self-determination using other dividing lines works very well, too. Sarah and Chris found that the way they looked at the world not only contributed to their relationship, but it provided a way to divide the work.

SARAH: Chris is the organizer and the planner and getting the nitty-gritty things of life done.

CHRIS [laughing]: I am? Oh, I thought you were that.

S: And, I look at it from a different point of view, it's spiritual, it's emotional.

Two of the couples have definite divisions when it comes to handling the finances—one partner is simply befuddled and perhaps a bit intimidated by the thought of budgeting and paying the bills, while the other is much more focused on the details, and that line just isn't crossed.

ELAINE: I think we each lead.

LISA: Yeah, we need to lead. And there are things that I'm really good at, and there are things that she's really good at, and we've learned, I mean if somebody needs to be yelled at, I'm good at that. I do that for a living and so it's like, dealing with contractors, making appointments, yakking at friends, I mean, that's just something I do well.

E: OK, and that's part of your cover. We couldn't buy this house together because it's going in the legal news. So she is perceived as the owner of the house, so she's the one that has to do all that stuff. And, for a while, that made me angry but I like it. . . . It's real nice to say, "You need to call."

It's like my cleaning up the clutter in the house and taking care of the house. I'm more willing to do that and, in some ways, that's traditional because she takes care of the money clutter. I am horrible at money. My father was very abusive when it came to money. I can't do it; plus, I'm dyslexic. So, she does all the money management.

And it's fair. I clean up this clutter, she cleans up the financial clutter. And she feels more in control of that, which she needs. And I feel more in control of this, which I need. So, that works. . . . It's more the way our personalities fit together.

L: . . . And then when it didn't work anymore because our lives have changed in certain ways, re-creating it; and we're really good at just negotiating and renegotiating and . . . And neither one of us has said, "OK, this doesn't fit any more." Maybe we've had a few fights first and there's like, bing, we're fighting, and then we'll sit and talk about it. And one of the things we've talked about is you cutting that back, the hours, and being here more because it really adds to our quality of life.

E: If I can be here on a Thursday and a Friday and I've got all the errands run and the shopping done and all of that stuff, I'm more sane because I haven't been dealing with other people's stress. And then, we've got the weekend. And she doesn't have to attend to anyone. Except to call the contractors.

L: . . . And, Elaine loves her practice and I know she doesn't want to give it up by any stretch of the imagination or would I want her to, but the thought of her working, you know, only three days a week, really appeals to me and I think it would work.

E: And I never would have thought that, what I had to learn in therapy was my mother and my sister were so stereotypical. And really wanted me to be that way. And, I fought it so hard that I wouldn't even be who I was. And I'm finding that I very much, I like taking care of our home. I like doing that, and I like taking care of her.

L: I mean, she's so good at this stuff.

E: I decorate.

L: . . . Around the house. I can appreciate it, but I can't do it. And she'll, we'll get something and I'll say, "You figure out where to put it." And then she'll put it in the perfect place. And I just love that. And, then, there's other things that I really do well.

E: Um hmmm.

L: Yeah.

E: She does [laughing].

L: I'm good at being real, at being real assertive with people.

E: Yes, you are.

Sandy and Rita find they have different attitudes toward money and handling their finances, almost the difference of the ant working steadily through the summer to accumulate enough for winter, while the grasshopper plays and lollygags until it's almost too late.

And, because their attitudes are so fundamentally different, they knew they needed some help in resolving how money would be handled.

SANDY: Therapy.

RITA: Yes.

S: We went to joint therapy because we were having problems with it. She was working, she had her money. I was working. I had my money. I had more money, so I paid a lot of the big bills.

And mostly for living and stuff, and then she paid, like her car and her car insurance and all her personal stuff. And then, even after you quit your job, I was still handling all the money at first, wasn't I?

R: I think so, most of it.

S: OK, so I would, I would pay all the bills. She never knew how much money I had in what account. She just never looked at anything. I didn't know she was interested.

R: And you would complain about not having the time to take care of all the bills. And I was, on the other hand, what about me? Why don't I take on some of this responsibility? I have the time, I can write out the bills. I can do that.

S: And she's very organized. It was really hard for me to give that up because I was used to handling all the money, doing everything. So we went to joint counseling about it and talked about it and I don't remember why I wanted to do all that, because now I bring my check home and sign it and give it to Rita.

R: It works.

S: It's much easier.

R: Well, you didn't know that I could be responsible with it.

S: OK, we had trouble with that, too. I'm a saver, she's a spender.

R: On other people.

S: On other people. Yeah, she likes to spend money on other people. So, I thought, I give her this check, she's going to blow it [laughs]. And at first, after she quit her job, I had all the bills plus then she had, a portion, I hate calling it an allowance, but she had money that was her personal money besides all the bills. I paid all the bills and wrote a check to her for her personal money and it was fine.

Their wildly differing attitudes about money and how the finances might be handled made them both look into the past and define how each lived before they became a couple.

RITA: Let's see . . . live for today, party, party, and give away as much as you can and still be able to make the rent and your car payment. That was pretty much it. So that's what she saw in me and I saw in her tight, tight, frugal, frugal. So, we both made big progress in this area because I've been extremely responsible with our budget and lots of bills and twenty-five checks a month that I have to send out. And it's a good feeling, having some responsibility and it's good knowing you don't have to do it because you don't really have the time to do it and I do. It's no big deal by me. It's not an issue.

SANDY: And we have joint money, part of the check is joint money and then we each have personal money, so the joint money's for joint stuff and the personal money, you know, if you want to give it away, that's fine. It's an ongoing thing.

R: And I think because we have money, that that affects my feeling about it. I can say, I don't need any of these material things. I would be fine without any of these material things and I have pretty much any money that I want, so that's easy to say that. But I don't really know if I was without if I could say that.

I want to really believe that and I want to be that "live simply so that others may simply live," and I look around and I say, what the heck did you spend two hundred dollars on that basket for, then?

So, it's kind of a strange thing. I think that part of the story for me will probably always be changing. And our finances will probably always be changing. Get richer! She brought home the pension statement tonight . . .

REFLECTIONS

There is no doubt—the art of negotiation is important. Whether it concerns chores around the house, money management or how out one is, negotiating with your partner is crucial to the relationship.

Communication and negotiation go hand-in-hand. They are such simple words, yet they are the building blocks of a relationship, and as such, might require the most attention. It is essential to any relationship that partners be able to talk to one another. Yes, there might be arguments but there might also be a longer, more fulfilling relationship.

These women talk to their partners about things that have an impact on their lives on a daily basis. There is no guide for the division of labor between partners in a same-sex relationship, so it can be made an equitable division, based on likes and dislikes, time and convenience. They have found the freedom, insight, and wisdom to recognize when they should sit down and talk—to each other, friends, individual therapists, or couples therapists. These people can help the couple co-construct the unfolding story of their relationship.

None of these women wishes to be like her parents. Some women believe their fathers were controlling, some have felt controlled in previous relationships. The women know what they don't want, but without role models, it is difficult to know what to want. Often, they default to one of two extremes—a relationship similar to that of their parents or one that they think of as ideal. Sometimes, women simply aren't aware they are being like their parents. Other times, they recognize the relationships and are determined to be different. Sandy and Rita talk of the difficulty of not imposing the thought of an ideal relationship on their partner and on their relationship. They also speak of the importance of actively attending to one another.

Communication, negotiation, and seeking help to co-construct a narrative help create stories of the relationship in which the partners are more equal and respectful of one another. And, these help avoid aspiring to an ideal that is not attainable, nor healthy.

Women find that shared interests add to the intensity of the relationship. The women bring certain interests to the relationship and if they spend time together doing things, it strengthens their bond. Lisa and Elaine tell how they share emotional intensity and passion, as well as interests in activities. And they point out that their differences are complementary and help strengthen their relationship. Chris and Sarah tell how their differences help them achieve their common goals, such as their work in the women's community and their bed-and-breakfast enterprise. It is not only the emotion, the way of being two women together, but that the shared interests add to time spent together . . . a growing of the intensity.

Enmeshment? No. A look under the surface shows that the strength of the bond between two women, not the enveloping of one within the other, is the key to a successful relationship. Each woman names common goals and shared values and is able to appreciate and respect the differences her partner brings to the relationship. Women relate to one another differently than men and women relate to one another. One can hear the difference and know when women are enmeshed and when women are in a loving, fulfilling relationship.

As the relationship deepens, it can take women into unknown territory and there might be stories of fear and anxiety that a relationship is ending. As women grow and change, they might develop new interests that their partners do not share. This does not mean that one is leaving the relationship, nor is it a signal for separation. Rather, it should prompt more communication and negotiation so the partners can pursue their separate interests.

These women have discovered the importance of taking the time to be in their community, to develop those bonds and explore shared interests outside of their relationship. No one can go it alone. A lesbian couple is never "just the couple." It is the couple in the context of its community.

These women see their similarities and their differences and are respectful of them. They also see the possibilities in their partners. These set foundations for the construction of their stories.

There are so many ways to tell a story. A woman, even when in a relationship, might choose to tell the story herself. She might defer and let her partner relate the tales. They might take turns, filling in details and advancing the story. They might tell the story to the interviewer, to a silently turning tape recorder or to one another, without a thought as to who might be in the room with them.

The telling might be thought of as a performance. And, the manner of performance is affected by whether it is for a general audience or a private one. A general audience, in these instances, might be society at large. This would mean taking into account all the constraints, restrictions, and/or freedoms one finds within that society. Thus, the stories themselves would be affected; the couples would shape their narratives to conform with the face they show the world.

The narratives also are shaped and might take some meaning from the ways they affect listeners. The narratives can illuminate a theme or a moral to the story, causing a listener to ponder relationships. They may resonate with truths that reflect in the listener's stories.

WE ARE OFF THE CLOCK

Not one of the stories told by these women follows strict, chronological order. Yes, the events of their lives can be placed on a time line, yet as history shows us time and again, events might be best understood with the perspective of time. And, an event that comes days, months, or even years later might cast preceding events in a new light. It takes all of our past to bring us to the present, and it probably will take the future to help us explain everything that will have happened. These women, in telling their stories, rearrange the events, re-sort the chapters according to meaning, rather than a clock or calendar. These are episodic narratives, woven by theme rather than time.

An example comes from Lisa and Elaine's conversations; they tell of their first night together. The women speak of a past event, and move to a discussion in the present about that event. Then they talk about what might occur in the future, but that hypothetical situation is not directly related to their story of their first night together.

LISA: I'll never forget the first night that we spent together. And we got up the next morning. I mean, I will never forget the way she looked that night, where we were standing, and it was just a lot of things. I could see the freckles across her nose and there was just a soft quality in the eyes and it was a real thing and a real genuine quality and . . . I realized that this was somebody that was really present. . . . And was not just hearing me but was actually feeling me and was picking up on that. . . . More sense than impression or anything.

ELAINE: And I didn't throw you out.

L: No, you didn't throw me out. You know . . . it was just, she and I are both really deep-feeling people. We tend to work from our guts first and we both are highly intuitive about things. You know, both of us could be in a restaurant and somebody could be fighting off across the room quietly and we would know it.

While the text of the stories might bend time, often the photos the couples choose to document their life are presented in chronological order. Whereas the text of the story is much more malleable and given to skipping about a time line, photos are concrete documents; they can be rearranged, but the images are frozen in a moment.

Marge and Jill have some photos depicting what happened when Marge came out to her family. They tell how Marge went home for the holidays and told her parents that she is a lesbian. Their pictures show Jill participating in Marge's family's life, such as playing computer games. But after the trip home, during which Marge came out to her parents, there are no more pictures of Jill with Marge's parents and family.

MARGE: They were at my parents' house. See, we used to go over there . . .

JILL: There I am. There we are playing [a computer game].

M: That's my mom. That was the house where I went over there to come out and they were working on fixing curtains and blinds in their bedroom. . . . And, oh, even my mom was so dysfunctional after I came out, crying, all this stuff's going on and I was telling them other stuff that happened to me in college and everything. . . . My stepfather wasn't shocked and he just said, "I just don't want Jill in this house ever again." . . . So, we're walking out, my mom's like, "Now, do you like the curtains in the dining room?"

M: "I made these curtains. What do you think?"

A couple's story can change and be changed. A story can be given deeper meaning, even a different meaning. And, the narrative also allows the teller to speculate on what might be. An example is a story of what retirement might be like for Sandy and Rita.

SANDY: But see, I've been planning retirement since my first day on the job (laughing). . . . So, well, I read all kinds of books on the subject. I plan on retiring early, but I really don't. It's like I think I'll get to the point where I'm able to retire and I'll probably want to keep working for a while longer. So I think it's got to be a hard time for me. And I think it will be a hard time for Rita because she's going to have to put up with me.

RITA: And you know, there are always options. . . . There are all kinds of options in anything and if we can just look at all those options that we have, we'll be OK.

Another example of time travel in narratives is Sarah and Chris's conversation about their future, particularly with regard to their physical health.

CHRIS: We're building more of a substantial community here beyond the bed and breakfast, a women's community. And I think that as that continues to happen, we get more long-term residents, maybe people who come once or twice every month . . . and are part of our household more than guests, I'd have to say. And as that happens more and more, we build up a reservoir, resources and support for us. I think that, most likely in the scheme of things, Jane will die before us. That will make the founding changes.

SARAH: And I will die before you.

C: No. Sarah has promised that she will not die before me because I would be at a total loss. She doesn't want that to happen.

The couples' narratives might be about a single moment in the past, or they might sweep across dimensions to infuse meaning. The words travel across time. Each of the couples tells stories in a collaborative manner. Lisa and Elaine use this form when they review their photographs, which remind them of a sailing trip.

ELAINE: And that was our last big sail last year. We were sailing to an island. And that was the furthest we'd sailed last year. Um, this is California after the election. And then this . . .

LISA: That's a lake and that's right before one of the big bike trips we took right before I ran for election. I was depressed there. I was real sad because I knew I was giving up my life for about eighteen months.

E: Yeah, and we were watching the regatta that you can't see.

L: And it was the fall of 1991.

There are times during the conversations that the women take turns answering a question. Chris and Sarah ponder what sort of a title could be used for their relationship.

SARAH: I know, without giving a title.

CHRIS: What's that? The saying . . . Long lasting.

S: I don't ever see Chris either in this life or any other life . . . titled. I don't know how to title that. . . . In so many ways, we're intermingled and yet get so much out of one person . . .

C: I don't know if I know either. We're together and we're very close together. We're not in any sense of the word I don't believe, enmeshed. But the title of a book or a movie. Oh, keepin' on, keepin' on. How's that?

S: That's fine.

Partners also have no problem asking one another for clarification or deeper explanations. They do not assume one another to be mind readers. When Marge and Jill talk, Jill refers to their relationship as normal. She then clarifies her use of that description for Marge:

JILL: I guess stability, like we're very stable, a stable relationship. . . . Versus divorce and like, constantly digging.

MARGE: Yeah. . . . Because you used it in this context the way you always use it, abnormal is homosexual and normal is heterosexual. . . . but you mean normal as in all couples straight or gay, we're not divorcing or dysfunctional, we're a couple.

When they are asked for a title that would sum up their relationship, Jill defers to Marge.

JILL: [Laughing] A creative riddle.

MARGE: I would say, I feel solid.

J: And we work hard to maintain that.

M: To describe our relationship, or . . . ?

J: You're usually pretty good with that stuff [laughing again].

M: I know, I can't think of . . .

J: Think of a good song.

Finally, at Jill's suggestion, she and Marge agreed that "respect" would be the ultimate description of their relationship and Aretha Franklin's song by that title tells it all.

On some occasions, each of the couples recounts stories to one another, sharing with one another once again the feelings of the moment, in the moment. This happens when Rita and Sandy talk about their commitment ceremony and how they fed cake to each other.

RITA: I thought it was fun. It wasn't real meaningful, it wasn't gaggy.

SANDY: The cake thing?

R: I mean the ceremony was meaningful.

S: No, I'm talking about the cake thing.

R: I'm talking about the cake thing.

The women know that their stories are going out to larger audiences. And yet, they tell their stories in an intimate manner. Only once do any of the women address that larger audience, and only in a peripheral way, such as when Elaine and Lisa discuss what they "tell people."

ELAINE: I don't know. What do we usually tell people? We usually tell them how long we've been together. Well, we usually tell them we've been together about ten and a half years, and um, she chased me for ten months. Yes.

LISA: You'd tell them that?

This is the one instance in which any of the stories is addressed to a larger group and while it does acknowledge others, the story still is told one to the other.

THEN, NOW, WHEN?

Each couple tells stories by placing events in three phases of time: as a past experience, present interaction, or future possibility. This is to be expected, because all the women are still in the process of writing their stories as couples, they are in the process of their relationships.

Elaine and Lisa revisited the past when telling of one of their dates early in their relationship.

ELAINE: And I go, "Well, why don't I just go with it and see what happens." It's like Joan Fontaine meets Mickey Mantle or something like that.

LISA: Oh, you're so silly.

E: I take her to the ballet. . . . I pick her up. She's got on a ski jacket. I'm like, "Oh, my god, she's got on a ski jacket."

L: I'm thirty, I'm a jock. I don't care.

E: And I've been with a woman who had a coat for every occasion, you know, and it's like "She's got on a ski jacket. OK." I told her, I said I knew she was a diamond in the rough, you know.

L: It was, I mean, because she wasn't really all that attracted to me. And I thought she was really neat and it was just like, I mean, I was younger. I was, I'm not horribly feminine . . . and I played softball, and I was a jock.

Often, the women would turn to one another in the midst of a story, and speak to one another in the present. This happens as Sandy wonders if there is anything else to tell of her relationship with Rita.

SANDY: I guess the only other thing that I wanted to say and I didn't even know I wanted to say it until you asked that, was, it's an individual thing but definitely impacts on the relationship. And, um, I was sexually abused by my grandfather and that's why I'm in group therapy. It's a group for women who've been sexually abused.

And, so that's really impacted our relationship, but it's something I've been working on and I'm doing OK. I'm doing OK and I think as long as I, you know, work it out, we're going to be fine. So it's impacted our relationship but because of all the therapy that we've done, we've worked through it. And I'll keep working on that until it's OK.

RITA: And maybe I'll be able to work on mine someday.

And they smiled at each other.

The couples just as easily speak of what might be, telling a story of what they see as their future. Marge and Jill talked about watching their girl grow up.

MARGE: Um, I know that in the future we probably won't, like the future I'm thinking of, we have not as yet achieved our final goal in life, hopefully. I mean, we won't be at that point where we won't be finished with the jobs we have to do, but we will be at a point where I'm not going to be worried about whether I have a job for the next year. For me, I'm talking.

JILL: OK.

M: Elizabeth [their daughter] will be older and in school, private school. But I see us all together and maybe another one. Who knows? . . . Oh, gee, grandchildren and there will be a little picture . . . no, I'll live a long time.

J: God, I'd hope so.

They share a laugh.

M: What are you thinking? So you're not going to say a title or are we going to get together?

There is a long silence.

J: I don't know. I'm going to have to ponder that one.

M: Do you see us all in the future together, though?

J: Yes, I do.

Sarah and Chris, who have built a community of women and extended themselves to those women, believe the future holds the promise of an extended family, all caring for one another and the land.

CHRIS: I think aging is going to affect us in our relationship so, I don't even exactly know how that really is, but it's sort of scary to me. Because you can't do the things, can't do as much of the things that you used to do and how you find ways to adapt and still get things done. But I think we've built a pretty good foundation for that. You know, it's like doing the yard work, that's normally what Sarah will be doing in March. We had somebody here in February working and it's great. So I think, in terms of the future, that's a big, big piece to deal with is the aging process. And Sarah's ten years older than I am, at least chronologically.

SARAH: And basically because we have a seventy-eight-year-old member of our household, caretaking is probably going to be in our future, too. And that's something we made a commitment to, so that could change the pattern. Most of the time, I physically get most of the caretaking of this place done myself with help from Chris on the weekends.

C: Well, then Jane has been, up until the last couple years, a major contributor to stuff that had to get done around here. And that's changed, majorly.

S: She does very little at all anymore. So, if we continue this place and continue the services we offer, there has to be some other means of support. And I think it's hard when you're caught up in the nitty-gritty of everyday life, of stuff that just has to be done. To find time to maintain and continue our couple's story. . . . To say that that's a priority.

C: We're building more of a substantial community here beyond the bed and breakfast, a women's community. We'll keep looking for a younger woman. Maybe I'll have some younger women to, to come on and sort of . . . like what we did with Jane.

S: Most of the younger women themselves need us to take care of them. I'd like to change that mode. . . . Well, one of the things we have, uh, two work weekends à year. That's one of the things that can structurally change, too. Doing major portions of bringing wood in and starting gardens in the spring.

C: We have, too, we've had several long-term residents who were here for two months, I think. We've had varying degrees of success with that. Some were real successful and others a lot more work than we wanted. We've gotten mature in, I think maybe we'll be a little more cautious in choosing them, but usually that's another way of being supportive.

Still, the problems of keeping up while getting older pale in light of the basic reasons Sarah and Chris build community.

CHRIS: I think over time our relationship has grown because of our being around so many women. Hearing their stories. And I'm a big one for hearing people's stories. And I think everyone has a story to tell. I love to hear 'em.

SARAH: So much of the energy that they put out and then leave with this land, even when they're not here, their energy is still a part of this land.

Chris and Sarah's friend easily defines and appreciates their role in their community and talks of how that is evolving, how it shapes their relationship, and how she sees the future playing out.

FRIEND: When I talk about the evolution of their relationship, I really am talking now about the evolution of their vision. And how that's grown and how they are giving more, it's how, it's like any vision, you know. You've got the vision and it's a big vision and it's great and it's wonderful and you go for it and then reality starts to shape it a little bit, you know, how women are with each other. We have not learned to dwell with each other.

We can't be trusted and that affects the vision you want to have about women and your life with women. So, I think that they have learned a lot over the last few years about what can happen and sort of what's out there if you open yourself and say, "I want, I'm committed to living in the community . . ." So, real cases are going to show up and, what does that mean? What does that mean to you individually and your energy and how that energy can be really sucked dry? And what does that mean to your vision, and how's that going to temper perhaps what you want to do? So that's the biggest thing that I've seen. Oh, it's definitely connected.

I can't talk about Chris and Sarah without talking about what they dream and they talk about it all the time. I mean, that's something you share, that's something you have in common and it's something that excites them and keeps their juices going. I just don't ever see them ever retiring down on the farm.

It would be shocking to me. However, I do see them tempering their desire for all women with what they personally can extend. I mean, you might want to have a wonderful world for all women but you've got to have those women help.

And so, I think they're getting very smart about what needs to happen and how much needs to come from everybody. I mean, I think Chris more so than Sarah, and I think this is true of most of us. I think they figure they can do it all themselves, they can take care of the world and they can't.

Still, there is one specific wish their friend has for Chris and Sarah.

FRIEND: That they keep on going like they're going and that their dream comes true and that they have lots of years together and I hope to be a part of that. You know, I hope that I will be definitely an intimate part of that. It's a pretty big wish. They've got pretty big ideas. And I hope they all happen.

IT COMES UP IN CONVERSATION

All four couples travel through time to give meaning to their narratives. What is past might be prologue, but it is not presented in that order, nor is the past given breadth and depth of meaning until the present, or even the future. And, as with all storytellers, the women remain firmly planted in the present when discussing the past, the present, and/or the future.

Marge and Jill discuss a past event that has implications for the present and the future, while relating to each other and their daughter in the present.

JILL: I guess I always saw like, I mean even since I was little I always saw myself married to a man and definitely with kids. That didn't change until I met Marge. And I always knew that I would never settle for anything less. I would never settle for just maintaining a status quo. . . .

So I always knew that whatever relationship I ended up in, I definitely would not put up with any kind of situation that was unhealthy or that I would not be respected or that could be abusive.

[Talking to the baby] . . . And, oh, hi.

I think that I just always knew that. . . . You know, I dated a guy one time, had dated for a year and then he had made some pretty crass remarks to me and I was just like, "Well, you're out of here." I just wasn't willing to settle and overlook those types of qualities in order just to be with somebody.

MARGE [looking at Jill, talking about their daughter]: Do you want me to take her? Or do you?

Chris and Sarah speak in turn, talking of past relationships and how they affect what they want from one another. What they want is given meaning by their former relationships and their conversation moves easily from past to present.

SARAH: . . . We explore ideas. We build on, it's like Chris when she develops programs for her work . . . you sit down and you brainstorm, and I think we do that in this relationship. We sit down and one of us will have the idea and we'll toss it off the other person.

CHRIS: We also, in the early years, I'd say like the first five years, there were times we did counseling, couples counseling. We had both been in really pretty bad relationships and so we knew what we didn't want it to be like.

REFLECTIONS

The women tell their stories very much as a conversation, and in these conversations, it is clear that all four couples are in the process of their relationships. They do not know how things will end, they can only speculate. So, without the perspective of time and distance, they are trying to make sense of events, some quite vague, that are not yet completed.

The women eschew linear thought when telling their stories, moving seamlessly through the telling of a past event, to a current interaction, to a future possibility. Each woman is comfortable being in the middle chapters of her narrative, and that is reflected in how the stories are told. The women are in their homes, in warm and inviting atmospheres, telling the stories, laughing, crying, opening their homes and hearts to share their lives.

All four couples say they work on their relationships. They are intensely involved in the co-construction of their stories. These conversations show how, as individuals, they once told their stories, and how as a couple they have told their stories, and how they tell their stories now. The narrative is always undergoing reconstruction. As the women remove or rearrange or reinterpret parts of their story, the events unfolding in their lives every day prompt them to add to their narratives, to construct the story that has meaning for them now, in the middle of this process.

The women learn they must find a language to represent their experiences. The very matters that create meaning in their narratives and important issues have not been named. Language that already does not fit with women's lives is even more at odds with lesbians' lives and experiences. And so, the women search for and construct meaning out of the language they know. They allow for a translation of that language and search for new language that will best fit the stories they are trying to tell.

Oppression Hits Home

We can read its definition in the dictionary. *Oppress:* To crush or burden by abuse of power or authority; to burden spiritually or mentally as if by pressure.

We can know its definition by the act and its repercussions. Oppression can easily be seen in the lesbian community. Parents, family members, acquaintances, co-workers, the religious, people on the street—all have opinions as to the "normalcy" of same-gender couples and many are eager to share those opinions. The couples' class, social standing, education, work, friends, clothing, actions, and attitudes can be lightning rods. When those judgments are backed by numbers, authority, even repetition, oppression can result.

One reaction can be the construction of private and public narratives, the telling of one story for ourselves, the telling of another in public. It is a subtle and delicate distinction, for our telling must always touch the truth. Politics aside, no one should be expected to walk into the maw of nonacceptance, condemnation, even violence.

Among the areas in which these couples have been affected are careers, family, or even just living in the neighborhood. It is in these areas the women must decide: How to behave? There is the fear of family members turning their backs, losing a job, friends falling away, not being tolerated.

Often, oppression forces women in same-gender couples to act differently toward one another in public. It can be a question of physical safety or emotional stress or both. It can be a matter of comfort—one's idea of acceptable public displays of affection. Surroundings can have an impact. The couple that walks together on a downtown sidewalk at midday, keeping a discrete distance between themselves, might that night walk into a lesbian bar holding hands. Being in gay space can invite bolder, brasher, more colorful carriage; women do not fear eye contact, and they give little thought to being judged for their sexual orientation.

Sandy and Rita move among at least three environments: in public, among lesbians, and at home. Each environment elicits a different approach.

RITA: If you saw us at the mall, you'd probably think, "Oh, they're a couple of women that are friends." I mean, we wouldn't be holding hands, we wouldn't be kissing, we wouldn't be doing anything intimate. Just that, you know, they're friends and you'd only have an hour to do that because Sandy has a one-hour shopping limit. Whereas, if you meet us at the bar, if you'd be observing us at the bar, OK, we probably, well, we usually dance and . . . Sandy enjoys slow dancing, so she'd be slow dancing with me. I'd be . . .

SANDY: Fast dancing with me.

R: Disco.

S: I'm trying to hang on and she's trying to wiggle all around.

R: No, that's only some of the time. That's a real close intimate . . . situation for us because we usually kiss when we're slow dancing.

S: Well, that bar's different even from home. Like if we're playing pool at the bar, as opposed to playing pool here. Usually, we're real touchy, too. It's like the bar's a real touchy place.

R: But you're sillier here.

S: I'm sillier here.

R: Yeah, you'll really let loose. Like, I'd never seen you dance before in our basement—"Whoa, I like this!"

S: I like to dance, but I like to dance when it's just us. I'm kind of inhibited when I go out somewhere. I'm not inhibited here.

Other couples also make accommodations. While Lisa is a member of the yacht club, Elaine is admitted as a guest, despite their relationship. Lisa's first campaign involved a stand-in partner, a gay man.

Chris and Sarah have created a refuge that is very much women's land. All the couples maintain a story at home and a story in the world. And, their ways of being in the world are not always acknowledged or accepted in the public arena.

Chris and Sarah have their bed and breakfast in a rural area, where they can honor, cherish, guard, enjoy, and share their sense of the land. They keep it primarily women's land, limiting the number of men, so they choose their "public" carefully while building a community.

SARAH: We both lived in [a large city] for a time, then we came back to the land. Our story was majorly different then. We both had full-time jobs. . . . I think moving to the land [changed the story].

CHRIS: Oh, being around so many women. We spend fairly intensive time around an awful lot of women. Especially during the, you know, all winter long it's four to six a weekend and then during the summertime, we have twenty here or more. It's not that unusual. . . . I think, over time, our relationship has grown because of our being around so many women.

Because their community is chosen and because they have the option of remaining apart from the world at large, Sarah and Chris have built private and public narratives that are similar. They are the same with one another no matter who they are with, no matter where they are. A friend of theirs succinctly sums up that consistency: "My relationship to them as a couple is how they are in the community. How that couple presents itself in community, sustains community, builds community, sees community as important. It really is how, who they are as a couple and also as individuals."

Lisa and Elaine are selectively closeted. And their friend describes the consequences.

BRIDGET: This always makes me so sad, I can't imagine having the kind of relationship that they have and not being able to have a picture of Elaine on my desk. Of not being able to take Elaine to social professional functions. You know, I can't imagine when people are sitting around talking about things that they've done over the weekend with their family, to have to talk so anonymously. You know, they have a beautiful relationship and they have to keep it so hidden. And it's not like they're ashamed . . . they have a life together as a couple but I think Elaine is more out than Lisa, and for obvious reasons. But it pains me that they have something so wonderful and they can't showcase it, they can't put it out there and use it as a fine goddamned example of how well this works and how healthy it is and how good it can be for two people. . . . It's like this bright, shining star that can't come out.

Regardless of how out the couples are, the women speak of the importance of participation in the women's or lesbian community. For Rita and Sandy, that means regular vacations in Provincetown, Massachusetts, a town known for its acceptance of lesbian and gay women. They share some photographs that help define their relationship.

SANDY: Oh, that's in Provincetown.

RITA: The first year?

S: Yes, first year we went. We've been back every year since. We bought, we have two timeshares there.

Sarah and Chris, on the other hand, lean toward the Michigan Womyn's Music Festival. All the couples agreed that immersion in areas that feel safe for them allows them to gain strength to maintain and sustain their relationships.

Sandy and Rita, at first, did not think they had experienced oppression.

RITA: I think mostly because we're closeted most of the time and with most of our life.

SANDY: But, you know, it's so much a part of your life for so long, you get used to it. Maybe, maybe we're oppressed and we don't even feel it anymore because we've been oppressed for so long. I mean, there are some things that spark anger, and it's especially hard when we go to P-Town and when we come back or to Michigan and come back . . . back to the real world. But then after we get used to it again, it seems like it's OK again. But, yet right afterward, it's like real confining until we get used to it again.

We can touch in public and it's accepted. I mean just holding hands. Walking down the road in P-town holding hands or in Michigan or, you know, acting in a loving way, nothing bad, you know, I'm not jumping on top of her or anything, but just kiss her on the cheek or acting in a loving way. We can't do that safely . . .

R: Yeah, safe . . . Take off our shirt and we're not going to be raped. And know we're going to be safe. Just that, you know, walking around outside and holding hands.

S: I do sometimes wish I could hold her hand in the mall. I do wish I could hold her hand sometimes.

R: Well, I think in environments where we know that's OK, like when we were in Key West and we stayed at a hotel that only gay women were allowed to be there.

S: I mean, we were much more ourselves.

R: As opposed to walking down the street in . . . where you can't do that.

Lisa and Elaine, when first asked, also said they did not feel any oppression. However, they thought about it.

LISA: I think what was hard is, it's like we're two very well-educated, productive people. We make a lot of money, we pay a lot of taxes. I mean, we function in the world and everything that society as a rule would say that people should do, we do. You know, it's like Bridget. One of Bridget's jokes is at her wedding, we were the most conservative people there.

ELAINE: We're just strange.

L: And it's true in some ways. . . . I mean, we're really pretty fairly conservative in terms of how we approach the world and simply because of that one fact [being lesbian] . . . we're subjected to some person just treating you like you're less than human. . . . If you're going to weigh people's value in this world or what value a human being has in this world, it has nothing to do with anything.

So, in terms of how that affects us, whether it be the fact that she's invisible and all the different ways in which we hide our lives for me to function in my job, I think in some ways, it just keeps us tighter.

Chris and Sarah have felt oppression and their friend has watched it and how it has affected them.

FRIEND: I haven't met any of Chris's family and knew they have not been accepted by her family. . . . Sarah's family is, Sarah has had a lot of family strife. It's like family, family, family in the relationship, family, you know, taking care of her sister's daughters. Providing for family, watching out for family and not getting that respect back, not getting recognition back. And Sarah also is, this has been a family year for her. Anyway, all I know is that she's going through family stuff and continuing the journey of separating herself and her work from what her family thinks and feels, and doing a decent job of it, too. It's like, you know, I know who I am and they are who they are.

And that's their trip. But family has had a big effect on her, I think. Well, it has on Chris, too, but there's so much more. I get so much more of a sense of family in listening to Sarah, you know. Family's been present through a lot of her life and not in supportive ways. And she's been a supportive person. . . . Which really seems an injustice there.

Their friend also is aware of how the world reacts to their relationship.

FRIEND: You mean about being lesbians? They don't shout it . . . But they know people. Chris, this is something Chris would do. I mean, she'll talk to these people that come around and I think to myself, "Jesus, how can you stand it?" But she actually kind of gets a kick out of it. And she'll chat with the pump guy or this guy or that guy.

They know their neighbors. Chris wants to be a visible kind of gal, you know. She wants people to know she's there and who she is, but she doesn't say anything, so it's not like they hide at all. They know people but they don't go around yelling they're lesbians.

I mean, they make small concessions. They wear bathing suits, I think, when they swim with family [but not otherwise]. I don't think they make concessions about who they are.

For Marge and Jill, the birth of their daughter has been unique and earthshaking. The effort it took to have the baby, the effort it takes to raise her and provide for her future, and the fallout with the family all have had huge effects on their couple's narrative.

Marge and Jill went to a fertility specialist, who acted as if Jill were to be a single mother. And, the friend who told them of this specialist did not find that odd. In fact, the specialist demanded that as a single mother, Jill must undergo psychological screening.

JILL: I mean, we had been coupled for almost ten years when we had started getting pregnant. And that was not even, I mean, we had been coupled and monogamous longer than a lot of people had been in heterosexual marriages. So, that was really difficult for me because I felt that what we had gone through to stay committed to each other and build a relationship wasn't even honored or acknowledged. And here was someone [the friend] that I really cared about and respected and when I brought it up to her she said, "Well, he only requires it of single women." It's like she didn't even realize what she had said. And I said, "I'm not single."

Later, they spoke of the effect that their relationship and their baby has had on their families. Marge said she would visit her parents often.

MARGE: . . . And after I was honest with them, we don't see them anymore. It dwindled down to where I just saw my mother maybe three times a year and now I don't even see her.

JILL: OK, Marge's mom and I would go shopping, you know, just the two of us.

M: Well, when we gave her the book of, of our story, she just took it back. She did not want to read it. . . . Five years. That's a big change for us. It has been good and bad, because, I feel better not lying or trying to camouflage the story just to get along with them, and it's better because now, you don't have to worry about where you're going to go Christmas, or the different holidays. So, I mean I feel bad that they cannot accept it, but I'm not going to change my story to help them cope with it.

J: . . . And in the whole time I can't believe that a parent can totally reject a child. You know, I just, I still cannot fathom how that could be. Because I, we haven't seen Marge's stepdad for the entire time, for five years and Marge's mom would come and visit periodically, maybe twice a year. Um, until she found out we were having a baby and . . .

M: Well, she wanted to see the baby but not ever to let her, let my stepfather know anything about it and I'm not going to play those games with my child. I mean, it's not worth it to have mom come down and, and hide her, because someday she's going to understand what's going on and I just will not, I'd rather never see them again, than. . . .

J: See, I don't ever remember her wanting to see Elizabeth.

M: Right. That's what I mean, but if it, if [her stepfather] would have been out of town or something, she probably would have been able to come down. Like she said, "Oh well, I'll never let Frank know about it." You know, "What is it? A boy or a girl? Do you know yet?" and she seemed somewhat excited but then, I'm not going to keep secrets, which is part of the theme of their family, and I won't do that to my child. . . . So, that was a major change.

J: And my brother, my older brother, when he found out that I was pregnant, um, we haven't seen him ever since. And, I mean, he always loved Marge. You know, if we had any kind of family event and then by chance Marge wasn't there, which was rare, I would walk in and before he would even say hi to me, the first thing he'd

say is "Where's Marge?" But then when I told him that I was pregnant, you know what I mean, he does the old, "I'll never approve of
this and I'm not going to talk about this right now because I don't
want to say things I'm going to regret," and, oh, then he said, "I'll
call you when I'm ready to talk about it." And I said, "OK, fine."
And I haven't heard from him even though I had written to him
twice. . . . And finally, he did call when the holidays this year were
coming up because he thought he was going to see me, but we still
have not seen each other.

M: Well, I mean they have four kids that we used to play with all the
time, and we went down for one of Jill's nephews' birthday party
and brought Elizabeth. She was probably about four months old?
Three months old?

J: She was four months.

M: And we got out of the car, all the kids said, "Whose baby is that?"

J: So they hadn't even told their children that we'd had a baby. So I
think that that changed things.

The couples contrast the safe and welcoming atmospheres of lesbian spaces with the world they live in—home, with service people,
fellow workers, even relatives who are not aware of their relationship.
Rita and Sandy talk about this.

RITA: This morning, I was out at the cottage and I was waiting for the
furnace guy to come out. He showed up, it was a new guy. He
didn't know me and we were having a conversation; I found out
he's a cousin of my sister-in-law. And, you know, fifteen, twenty
minutes into the conversation, he asked me if I'm married. And I
said no. But I am. I'm married to her. I couldn't say, "Yeah, her
name is Sandy and we're lesbians," you know. That's just the way it
is for us. That's being in the closet. Although I wish society would
be OK enough and I could have said, "Yeah, I'm married and you'll
see her name on the check with mine." That's the real world here
for us.

I don't know how it really impacts us, other than we choose to spend time with our lesbian friends probably more than anyone else. Now, we go over to your family's and they accept us as a couple, but like we said before, we haven't talked about it.

SANDY: How has that impacted? I don't know because I don't know what would be different if they did know, or if, my impression if the world knew is all bad. So I don't want the world to know because I think it would be all bad stuff. I think maybe some people would accept us but the majority wouldn't. And there's lots of examples out there to show that they wouldn't.

Um, my family, I've never felt like I really, really need to tell them. And I know a lot of people do, and I think that's fine but I can't think of a good reason to do it. So, I'm still not going to. When I figure out a good reason that I feel like doing it, I will.

Rita and Sandy see the difference between their relationship and legally sanctioned marriage, and the difference that makes to them as a couple.

SANDY: Financially it would be so much easier if we were married, all the insurance stuff and the inheritance stuff. All that stuff's really important. But that's a major hassle. . . . You know, if one of us dies, the inheritance tax is terrible even though you try to do that kind of stuff (creating legal protections). And, it's not fair . . . we have to have separate insurance.

RITA: Well, last week when I met my brother and his wife . . . they were running a little late and I looked down the street and there they were, coming up, holding hands, walking down the sidewalk, and I thought "Gee, you know, they're lucky. I'd love to be doing that with her." There's no way, unless we're in P-Town or Michigan that we can do that. It's those little things.

The little things add up, eventually summing up the fact that lesbians, as outsiders in a heterocentrist society, often are not allowed to live freely.

Elaine and Lisa were faced with a major decision when Lisa first considered running for public office. The decision to run was made several years before the campaign, which lasted eighteen months.

ELAINE: And all of a sudden we had to do this, I had to go back into the closet after twenty years. And she had to be out there in the public eye.

LISA: And I mean, there were real hard parts to that . . . I'm really introverted by nature. And so I had to learn to splash and dash out there.

I remember when I made the decision to run for election. It was years, I mean it was five years before the race was actually run. And at that point, we made a decision to go on with that. And we really stopped, you know, being very visible at all. And it wasn't so bad as long as it was us together.

But then when it actually came to the time when we're doing this and, you know, I've got a gay male friend who's escorting me to places, OK? And, so it's Saturday night and I'm getting all dressed up and going out with him to play a straight person.

E: And they're getting lots of nice strokes.

L: And getting lots of nice strokes for, aren't they a beautiful couple, you know. And I mean, she was pissed. And, I can't blame her. And, I mean, it was really hard because all of a sudden our relationship didn't show, it didn't count, we couldn't talk about it, I was creating a persona that was completely separate from who we were together. And she's giving me time for that.

E: She was basically married to her campaign person for about a year and we just kind of, once we got that this is the way it's going to be, it was like, OK, then we could stop fighting it. And it's to the point that people eventually thought that she was with her campaign person, which cracked me up.

L: But it was one of the times when we had to do joint therapy together because she was so angry at me and I understood the anger but I didn't know what else to do.

E: . . . But also angry at the reasons why you had to do it. And it was really hard because all we had was each other to fight with.

L: And what was fascinating is what we did and I hadn't really thought about it before and I don't think you had either, but we went to see her therapist and she was saying what she had to say and I was saying what I had to say, and it was when I really was clear just how hurt she was about all of this, what I said was, "This is something I've wanted to do, but if it costs me the relationship, it's not worth the cost."

You know, I'm not doing this for me, I'm doing this because it'll double my salary, it'll double the amount of time we have for vacation. It will improve considerably our standard of living. And that's how I'm perceiving this, as a benefit for us as a couple. But if the cost is too high, I don't have to do this. I mean, I can just continue working the way I'm working, you know, we're getting by.

E: And it was like, dear God, I can't ask this woman to give up her, she shouldn't have to pick between a career and me. And I'm not the one that's going to make her choose that. You know, society is doing that. And, at that point, I said, "fine" and then I settled in.

L: And we just did it then, and it was much easier.

REFLECTIONS

All stories have influences, whether from within, from the past, from society, or from what one believes and/or assumes to be true. These couples' stories are heavily influenced by oppression. It determines how they construct their narratives as couples, how they are in this world. The stories also are affected by the couple's degree of being out.

Where does the oppression originate? What forms does it take? Can the women recognize it for what it is, and still embrace their value as human beings, loving women, contributing members of society?

All the couples discussed the impact of the experience of heterosexism. Two couples—Lisa and Elaine and Jill and Marge—elaborated on the effects it had on their narratives. Jill and Marge felt the effects most when they decided to have a child. They were not able to share their experiences or even tell people outside their circle that they had a child. Lisa and Elaine felt the impact in their careers.

There are several ways in which these women try to overcome the effects of oppression. They can remove themselves from the situation, surround themselves with support, refuse to acknowledge or engage the oppression, take legal action with wills, power of attorney, deeds and adoptions, or become activists. Each couple has found a place that is safe for them, but it seems that most find it necessary to travel to havens for same-gender couples.

Sometimes, the lesbians' invisibility is what allows them to be in this world. How else can they move in this world? Can they build community for support? Are they certain they can rely on one another? In varying degrees, the women can find comfort and solace in an oppressive world with friends, family, and the women's community.

The far-reaching impact of telling these stories can be seen in the reaction of one of the participants. The transcriber, who is accustomed to typing words without really absorbing them, was drawn into these narratives. These stories held the power to seep into her consciousness and she became a witness.

TERRY: This creation you and your participants have made needs to be told. And we Americans can preach about discrimination, especially about race and ethnicity, till we're blue in the face. I never realized there was this much discrimination for the nonheterosexual.

I can understand the inequality of life, specifically for women in a man's world. I apologize for bringing my life into your study, but this is the "real world" as you mentioned and I know what oppression/discrimination is all about. Listening to your participants' stories kept me grounded in some way. Maybe human beings could learn a few things about how to treat people and how to keep a relationship alive for a long time.

~~6~~ Every Story Has Influences

No story is created from nothing. Even the most gifted verbal alchemist cannot spin golden threads from thin air. There must be material. These couples share common material. Their stories come from past experiences, including early in their lives; society, including prejudice, oppression, and gender issues; and from their families of origin, ethnic background, culture, and families of choice.

Sarah and Chris again acknowledge how former relationships provide a direction for this one, even though at the beginning of this relationship, Chris did not look back.

CHRIS: And I just think we learned an awful lot from previous relationships and how not to do things. We just decided we weren't going to do that. That's the biggest part of it. Oh, I think jealousy was one of them. I had been with someone who was very jealous and very possessive and so, I knew for sure that it was not something I would tolerate at all. I didn't want any part of it.

And that was part of our earliest discussions and I had no meaning that I was going to go out and, you know, run around, . . . I just wanted to be, wanted to be assumed to be trusted. . . . If I was with, you know, went out to a movie with somebody else, or spent an evening with somebody else, I didn't want Sarah to be thinking that I was out, that I liked her any less, that there was anything wrong with our relationship, or that I was giving somebody else too much attention or whatever it was. I think that was important. I think it also has its turn side, that you always have to remember, and I've sometimes been guilty of this, um, in turn to give enough attention at home.

SARAH: I think that I had lost who I was. And I think the turning point for me was I would never do that again. I am who I am, stronger, and I would never ever have a lover that would deny me that.

THE OUTSIDE MATTERS

All the women say they have been influenced by people outside their relationships and by society because they are in same-gender couples. These people, family, friends, society, and culture help shape their stories.

Each couple has created legal documents that define their rights as members of the couple, as far as the law allows. If they have a serious illness, or one partner dies, the other will not be denied access to money, the house, or other assets.

The weight of society's norms affects Lisa and Elaine's story. When Lisa began her first campaign for public office, Elaine not only returned to the closet, but also watched as Lisa was publicly escorted by a gay man, with whom most assumed she was involved.

Jill and Marge felt the effects of society when they wanted to become mothers. They have told of their experience with a fertility specialist, who asked that Jill undergo psychological examination because he requires it for all of his "single patients." Of course, it is only the law that does not recognize their relationship; they had been a couple for almost ten years before deciding to have a child.

Jill and Marge recall family influences on how they divide their work at home.

MARGE: Where the boys don't do the dishes.

JILL: Yeah. My brothers never did the dishes. On Thanksgiving, on Christmas, after dinner they all went into the living room and watched football.

Early in their relationship, Marge and Jill did not believe it was possible for them to have a child. They assumed that the constraints of society would prevent it.

MARGE: I guess it was just when one person said, "Why couldn't you have one?" And then I just started thinking, "Well, why not?" And then I just started thinking, "Well, I wouldn't want to bring the child into this world with this, not a problem, but with this minority type thing against them." And that would be an awful thing to lay on a child, but then I realized by going through my old therapy, how my family was so dysfunctional. And I turned out halfway OK, so if there's just love, that would be even more than what I was raised with, so loving a child would be basically all it would need. As long as they knew that we loved them.

They also tell how having a baby changes their story.

MARGE: I just think it's pretty neat how love grows. Like, I've always loved Jill, but now it's like I love her even more, plus Elizabeth, it's just like expanding, the love and the caring and the respect and the sharing. Everything that made our relationship good is tripled.

Chris and Sarah also find that welcoming a child to their lives changes their story.

SARAH: Well, when my niece came, she came to say she was having a baby, which meant the child in our lives. Well, that obviously changed our lives. Chris had no intentions of ever feeling . . . and he's got her wrapped around his finger. He'll probably pretty much get what he wants. And, you know, it changes the dynamics when you have to deal with four instead of two or five instead of two.

As for Chris's family? She was rejected.

SARAH: How has that changed us as a couple?

CHRIS: I don't know, it drew us closer, I think. I don't know, you always think, "Well, you have your family to fall back on." But if you don't have your family to fall back on and you realize that you don't, it puts more, even more importance on the relationship.

PAST BECOMES PRESENT

The experiences each woman brings to the relationship influence the manner in which they construct their story as a couple.

SARAH: I'm working on a crown . . . and that crown is honored with the women in my life. And having worked on who these women are and there's been a number of women and they've not always been positive ones, but they've taught me major lessons in living and they've taught me the lessons that I have to learn from them makes up who I am this day.

And so I am who I am because I have learned those lessons that I had to learn that way. Some have been positive. A hell of a lot of them have been negative. But yet, I probably would do it again. I would hope that I don't have to.

Rita and Sandy also cite several of the same influences as the other couples, and add that counseling brings nuance and growth to their story.

SANDY: When we first entered into our relationship, I asked Rita that if we ever had a problem, if it would be OK with her if we went to counseling. That was like from the very beginning. So, at about year seven or eight, somewhere around there, um, we were having a problem with me being attracted to this other woman.

RITA: Year five.

S: Year five?

R: Yes.

S: Oh, OK, sorry. Um, and Rita was all upset about it and I didn't think it was any big deal because I wasn't going to act on it. So, we were upset enough that, I don't know, did we both decide at that time? I asked you if it would be OK if we went to counseling then and you said . . .

R: You asked me.

S: Yeah.

R: And I said yes.

These women also know how they developed their ideas about what a relationship should be.

SANDY: I think in growing up, it was determined culturally by what we observed in our culture and that would include how you see adults act, you know, in real life and also on television. An ideal couple when I was growing up was, you know, Ozzie and Harriet type people. Like, father and mother, mother at home, father there, you know, they love each other, they have two or four or six kids that always obey them.

[Rita rolls her eyes and they both laugh.]

SANDY: Well, there were eight kids in hers. Yeah, and you live happily ever after. You meet somebody, you fall in love and you live happily ever after. That's the ideal couple. It just happens. You don't, it's not like you have to work on it.

That was Sandy's idea of a perfect relationship, until she entered one and events made her wonder: This isn't easy . . . what's going on here?

RITA: I can only go by my role models. My parents certainly didn't work on their relationship. You're just, like you said, you see it on TV or you read about it. You don't see the work and the struggles and the compromise and the conflict resolution and all those things that really make the relationship. No way. No, you just don't. So I had no clue what was involved in, first of all, even thinking about going to counseling, then going to counseling and then doing the work and really communicating on levels that I had never seen before. We've really worked at talking and listening and talking about our feelings.

Friends have a hand in couples' stories. Rita had plans to move to Colorado when she met Sandy. Though there was a spark between them, Rita stuck with her plans.

SANDY: I think the first month, I was feeling very sexual and it was like, it was just fun time. But I still was kind of seeing another person, too, on a real superficial level. We'd never really gotten together but we had always said we wanted to, and I remember telling her if we were going to sleep together, we'd better do it now. And then we decided—she decided—that we weren't going to do that. So I wasn't feeling committed at all.

As for Rita. . .

SANDY: I was really interested and I really liked her and I thought there could, you know, potentially be a relationship there and I was feeling very strongly that way but we weren't committed to each other and so I didn't feel like we were really a couple.

RITA: I was going back to Colorado. That was the thing . . .

Even though they knew of the pending move, Sandy's friends treated Sandy and Rita as if they were a couple.

SANDY: If they invite one person, they invite the other to go along. . . . They'd call us up and say, you know, "Do you and Rita want to go someplace and do something?"

In the meantime, Rita's friends were treating the situation a bit differently.

RITA: My friends knew how interested I was in Sandy and so they'd always be asking me about her.

Rita, who was raised as a Roman Catholic, believed she would marry a man and have children. She dated men until she was twenty-three; that was when she realized she had a crush on a woman.

RITA: I mean, thinking of it as two women, um, grossed me out when I was a teenager. And then I was the woman having a crush on a woman, not knowing what was going on. I think I just had those feelings of attraction for her and then we were together physically and then I was around other lesbians and couples and I saw those couples and remember specifically seeing this couple that had been together for thirteen years, went to their house, saw all this stuff they had in their basement, activity things like sports stuff that they did together and these shelves were piled with all these activities and things and thinking, "That's really neat. Maybe I'll have that someday."

So that was a first thing in looking at me in a lesbian relationship and what it might be for me in the future as a lesbian and then a couple. I still had the feeling that I wanted the commitment and the ceremony and maybe a baby.

Ethnic background also plays a role in the co-construction of the couples' narratives. While Lisa and Elaine are openly affectionate with one another during conversations, they acknowledge that Lisa's "proper English upbringing" affects how they act in public—Lisa is more reserved. The other couples discuss ethnic background. Depending on the world view of their families of origin, a couple is either more open (public) or closed (private) in matters such as sexuality, emotional expression, and/or public displays of affection.

INFLUENCES FROM ALL AROUND

There are so many influences that cause us to shade our meanings, to obscure some facts when telling our stories. All four couples address the impact of society's definition of gender roles and the impact that has on the shaping of their narratives. Sandy tells of how she developed her idea of what a couple was.

SANDY: Part of it is like what you think of as an ideal couple. I mean, the good parts anyway. And that comes from a lot of different things. Part of it being the self-help books. I think part of it being just maybe on romantic ideas from books or television or whatever growing up of, you know, how it should be.

But I don't think religion at this point plays a real big, well, it depends on how you figure religion. Traditional religion, no. Different kinds of spirituality, probably yes. Probably part of it. That's a hard question.

Just the idea of a romantic couple, not necessarily heterosexual or homosexual, just a couple and how, you know, the right way to treat each other and the right way to feel about each other, it's kind of the idealized and that's what you strive for.

But, of all the time growing up, you have all that, even though that's not what your family is necessarily doing. But you know, any of the romance novels or any of that kind of stuff is ideal, get along all the time and feel wonderful and be sexual.

In similar manners, other couples tell of family or ethnic background and how they might have an effect on their stories. Lisa, who is of English descent, tells of the influence of her heritage on her story and on her and Elaine's story as a couple.

LISA: And I'm pretty square in some ways, you know . . . I was raised English. I mean, that's straight. And I've watched this woman just doing all kinds of outrageous pranks and jokes and stuff like that and I'd just be watching, laughing. But you know, my little kid was real attracted to this. And, so it was just like when we got together, it was just like I was really fascinated because she was the first person I'd been with that I believed was at least as smart as I was if not smarter. And I'm still not sure of that yet. Uh, but I mean somebody that could pace me every step of the way. I'd never had anybody that could keep up with me verbally. And who had an incredible passion for life.

Lisa also speaks of how she and Elaine see her ethnic background as having an impact on their story.

LISA: Very strong classic work ethic, a very strong sense of responsibility.

ELAINE: Yeah, yeah. That's true.

L: It's like, figure out your money, figure out what you're going to do with that money. . . . And I'm obsessive and she laughs, she says I'm nuts because of money.

E: And telling me about it.

L: I'm always trying to figure out what strokes the most, you know, and get the most out of it.

E: And she'd be down here with a legal pad and doing numbers and I'd be feeling bad and I finally figured out that she liked doing that. So it's OK.

L: . . . Most people do not express negative emotions. So it was a long time before I even had a chance to express anger in a relationship, to express anything that seemed to me other than, like if you're uncomfortable, you take a stiff upper lip. You just didn't do it, and so it was hard for me. I was scared to be able to . . . it was just like I wouldn't own it. And that was something that took some time. She lies, she's bawdy [laughing].

E: She's finally learning to do that a little bit.

They continue to speak of how Lisa was very controlled with her emotions. Elaine's ability to be loose has helped complement that, adding a more free expression of self that has brought humor into their lives.

ELAINE: I was going to say she's the best lay I've ever had. Thank you [laughing].

LISA: Oh, god! I told you! This is where my English part goes, "Oh shit! I don't believe she said that on tape."

REFLECTIONS

Each couple has constructed narratives based on early life experiences, previous relationships, the impact of oppression, and the influences of family of origin, and ethnic background, and society and culture at large. Each of these women entered a relationship with an idea of what being in a couple would mean, which comes from experiences in early life and in other relationships. When they entered this particular relationship and as they got to know their partners, they were writing their stories.

All the women have made it a point to explore the various influences on their lives and on their relationship. Then, they had to make a judgment: Good or bad? Allow it to remain influential? If not, how to change it? One partner can help the other recognize how the past affects them now. And, the partners also find resources outside their relationship in an effort to see and know what is influencing them now.

We have been able to share the public and private stories. The couples celebrate their lives together through their stories. Their narratives, as we read them, bring the couples to life. Rita and Sandy speak of what a wonder it would be if they could find a couple that has been together for thirty-five or forty years, for a role model.

RITA: I'm sure they're out there. I'm sure those couples are out there.

While Rita is sure and there is nothing to disprove her theory, there has been little to support it. The reason? Perhaps because Rita and Sandy are the role models, perhaps they are the women who share their stories so that others might find their voices.

What Do We Share?

What does it mean to share our stories?

It seems as natural as breathing to want to talk about our lives, our loves, plans and hopes, our disappointments and heartbreaks. Yet, as women in same-gender relationships, there are warnings, obstacles and roadblocks to such a natural desire to share. Because of the world in which we live, we must judge when it is safe to show ourselves completely, when it would be wise to keep quiet, and how it would be prudent to wait for acceptance to be revealed before revealing ourselves and our relationships. The sharing of our stories can make us vulnerable. And it can help bridge differences; in fact, telling our stories can show there is not that much difference at all.

What is it like to tell our stories?

LISA: I think the only thing I'd like to add, I think this has been really fun to do because I think that, that you can be aware of your relationship but it's really neat to relate it to somebody else.

I mean, it's sort of unique to be writing a history about yourself because it really sort of causes you, I mean, you sort of know where you're at in the here and now and where you've gotten to, but you forget your past in some ways, because you don't think about it continuously.

And, it was neat to be able to share that. I mean, it was neat for me yesterday to go to work and have Bridget talk a little bit about "Oh, god, I hope I didn't say anything that's going to piss you off." But I just sort of laughed and I said, "Do you love us?" And she said, "Yeah." And I said, "I wouldn't worry about it then, dear." And it was neat to hear her share because when she told me and we were talking in the parking lot and she said,

"You know, being able to talk about it caused me to really think about who you guys were and how I felt about you, and the one thing that really was clear to me was how intensely I care about you guys." And, I mean, that was nice. It's been a fun process.

ELAINE: It's been real nice seeing where we've come from in our relationship. And we've had a lot of couples really talk to us about the quality of our relationship.

The reflection of the relationships, the reminders of what is truly good, the thoughts of what had been, what is, and what could be also are apparent in the journals some of the women keep.

An example from Sandy's journal: I have been very sad lately. And working on this project and having the opportunity to reflect on the relationship I have has brightened my days. I was excited and eager for the interviews and time spent with you or the time Rita and I had together right after we were done with you. We have a wonderful relationship. I really love her.

Lisa and Elaine speak of how they describe their relationship to each other.

LISA: . . . And so it's really hard for me to, um, to allow myself to be softer and taken care of and held, and she's the first person in my life that showed me the qualities that caused me to want to be with people and trust them and feel that that wasn't going to be taken advantage of.

I'm a really intuitive person and so I feel things in people. And what I felt in her from the very beginning is these, a gentle spirit, a person that just didn't go out of their way to make other people uncomfortable.

Later in the conversation, Lisa again refers to intuition.

LISA: And so it's like we pick up things from other people and it's like we pick that up in each other somehow that, that, that absolute reliability.

ELAINE: We do that. I had a list of twenty-five items that the next woman I was with had to meet. She met all twenty-five. It was like, "son of a bitch!" Things as simple as likes to cuddle . . . is a wiggler . . . has been in therapy or would be in therapy.

In another conversation, Elaine speaks of how they are complementary, each bringing certain strengths to the relationship.

ELAINE: . . . There's rock and there's moss. When we went through her campaign, she kept referring to me as her rock. And she was just clinging and it was like, "Oh, moss. Moss clings to rock." So we figured there's rock and there's moss. And what I didn't tell you is the night before vacation, we found out the afternoon before we were leaving for Florida that I had this lump.

And we were up in the hallway and both of us just kind of walking around, spaced out. And she just, she came out of the bathroom and grabbed me and just held me and said, "Whatever you need, we're going to do it." And at that moment, I thought, "Wow, it's your turn to be this rock."

For a deeper look at the stories, we can turn to a friend or a family member—someone designated by the couples. Not only does the information confirm what the couples say, but it provides a peek into the more privately held narratives.

Chris and Sarah chose a friend whom they met at the Michigan Womyn's Music Festival. She spoke of the meeting, at which she immediately felt at ease.

FRIEND: A mutual friend I was walking with introduced us and immediately it was like, "Oh, do you want a beer, do you want a hamburger? Sit down, here's some potato salad." You know . . . a totally open, welcoming, sit down and share everything we have kind of a meeting.

. . . With Chris and Sarah, their relationship is not only who they are individually in community but their relationship is in community.

... I don't think people think of Chris and Sarah as just Chris and Sarah. I don't think they have for a long time. They think of it as the farm, they think of it as Chris and Sarah and Jane. They think of it as Chris. They think of it as Sarah. Sure, I say Chris and Sarah, but it's, there's always something more and if you don't, like if you just say Chris and Sarah, I think more often you'll find yourself saying "and Jane" or "and the farm" or "the farm." You know, there's a bigger thing there.

... And, if I were going to say to somebody, I have two friends, Chris and Sarah, immediately I would have to say "and Jane" and then I'd have to say a whole lot more. Not just about them, but about who they are, what they're creating, what they've done, how they've invited the community ...

Not only can their friend describe Chris and Sarah's relationship and their relationship to their community, she can look into the future.

FRIEND: ... You know, how I see other women functioning in this, is that either they go to work and come home and they have a pretty dead relationship, but the threat of independence is so great for women that they will stay in those relationships and, uh, we don't have a good model of community, we don't have a good model of living together in ways that are not restrictive, which is part of my work, just trying to figure that out.

And I think that Chris and Sarah have really done a very good job. I mean, Chris will say stuff like, "Oh, if anything ever happened to Sarah, I don't know what I would do." And I think you would say that about anyone you were close to. But I also know that Chris would be fine. It would be awful to lose a long-time friend. But she would not go psychotic, neither would Sarah.

... You know, it's a relationship, you begin to just count on certain things and you know someone very well and there's a familiarity about it and when that shifts dramatically, there is a lot of grieving that has to happen. And I think that for sure that would happen but I don't think they'd be destroyed. And I can't say that for any other relationship that I know. I'm talking about long-term relationships. I think that they would be much more devastated and the healing process would be curtailed much more. I think both Chris and Sarah would allow a healing process to happen.

Friends and family have different views of couples. Sandy's sister speaks easily of how she sees the relationship between Sandy and Rita.

SISTER: They're both very, I think, Rita's more sensitive than Sandy, but very caring of each other and very considerate of each other. I think they try not to make the other one unhappy. And they are always striving to keep a positive attitude in their relationship.

. . . Oh, I imagine just little things here and there. You know, just something little. Rita wanted, I know, a big barn built. So Sandy just, you know, like a project. So they just dove into that together. Something like that or, uh, I know they plan. They have a plan they follow just for maintenance of different things. . . . And they kind of build that together and they sit down and talk it over, I'm sure. And they seem to plan ahead together, doing things together. Building their home and their relationship, I'm sure, but I was trying to think of more specific things.

When you're around them, you get the sense of, um, they know what each other's thinking. I don't know, they've just, I guess been together long enough that you feel very comfortable with it.

Sandy's sister has known of Sandy's sexual orientation for some time and says, as Sandy does, that their family accepts Sandy and Rita as a couple but the family members don't talk about it.

Elaine and Lisa chose a friend who met Lisa through work and became friends with both. This provides her a chance to talk about her relationship with them, and how she views their relationship with one another. And, because she is planning to move, this conversation helps her put the value and wonder of their friendship in perspective.

BRIDGET: My husband is buddies with Lisa. And he, before he knew Lisa and Elaine, was probably homophobic. He was a farm boy made good. And, uh, very basic. And he knew that I spent a lot of time with the two of them and eventually it was we were going to do things as a couple. And I told him and he was like "Oh, shit, what's up with this?" And then, as we started to spend time together, he really liked them. And Elaine is my counterpart.

Elaine has some Southern history and roots. And I'm from the South and Elaine and I can be bad little Southern girls together and just giggle and laugh and we can tease. And, and it's sexual sometimes. Um, Elaine and I can tease Stan and Lisa like that and just have a hoot at it.

And I love them, but I love them in a very different way. Lisa and I, our relationship has a lot more of what I would call "edges" to it, because we have to deal with each other professionally and we have hard issues we have to hammer out. And we don't always agree. And so sometimes we can be very intense together. And focused. And with Elaine, it's always kindness. It's always softness. It's always love and warmth and, you know, when there have been times when I was hurting, she's been so sweet to me. And nurturing.

Still, their friend says that the relationship is "pretty no holds barred."

BRIDGET: We went out to eat three or four weeks ago and we were drinking and I was eating ribs and I had barbecue sauce all over my fingers and, um, I taunted Lisa until she sucked my fingers and it was a mistake on my part [laughing]. Because I had no idea what it would be like [laughing]. And it was like all of a sudden, my whole body was in her mouth and I'm just sitting there, my face turned purple and Elaine is going "I want one! I want one!" And I said, "I can't do this anymore."

I've told Stan about half-joking, um, I said, "If you leave me, that's it. I give up on men. I'm jumping the fence." And there was a time when I was divorced and I wasn't dating and I wasn't active sexually at all for a very long time and I didn't want to be.

And I liked strong women. That I was afraid that I was a lesbian. And Lisa would say, "Now, you don't have to worry. You like men, trust me." But I am a nondiscriminate flirt.

Elaine and Lisa form a couples' role model.

BRIDGET: I remember telling Stan when he wanted to get married and I never wanted to be married again, you know, I would say to him, "I only know one couple that has what I would consider a satisfying, healthy relationship. And it's not a man and a woman."

Their friend sees, firsthand and often, how Lisa and Elaine complement each other's strengths.

BRIDGET: Lisa couldn't do what she does without Elaine, no slight to Lisa intended. And Lisa wouldn't, she goes home and gets recharged. She goes home and she gets her heart and soul repaired. And she gets patched up to come back. If she didn't have Elaine or she didn't have that kind of a relationship, this would eat her alive.

It is clear from conversations with Bridget that Elaine and Lisa always present themselves as a couple when they are with her.

BRIDGET: . . . . I think Lisa would be lost without her. She is the salt of the Earth for Lisa. She is all the softness that Lisa, Lisa borrows her softness. And I think Elaine borrows Lisa's strength.

No, I can't imagine, not ever, and I would go to the front line to honor and defend and protect the integrity and the rightness of their relationship if anybody ever questioned it.

Sandy's sister tells how she sees Sandy and Rita as a couple.

SISTER: I think they both feel very comfortable coming, well, probably once a month on Sundays we all get together at Mom's. We go every other Sunday. Sandy doesn't go quite as often, but, and Rita always comes and Rita's always at our Christmas. . . . She doesn't go to her family's much any more.

Sandy's sister says she doesn't know many details of Sandy and Rita's life as a couple.

SANDY: Um, my family, even though, a lot of my family members don't know that I'm a lesbian, officially [laughing] . . . . My sister does, my brother does, but it hasn't been talked about, but it doesn't really matter. . . . The family members we hang around with accept us as a couple, also.

Sarah and Chris define themselves as a couple, and as members of a much larger group of women.

CHRIS: . . . It's fine to be known as a couple . . . it's fine. It's not an all-important thing with me. I know that I'm in an ongoing relationship and I assume others do, too, but for us, I think it's maybe a little different from people who are not involved as intimately as we are in the women's community. We really are involved very heavily and play major roles and have major responsibilities in that community as individuals.

Their friends and members of the larger women's community also have no doubt that Chris and Sarah are a couple, though not in what they see as the usual sense.

FRIEND: The things I have to say most about their relationship that I think has sustaining qualities is how they're not like a couple . . . First of all, they're not insular. They are always extending, they are always open. New people come in and go. They allow themselves to have, I think, intimate, now I don't think sexual relationships are intimate, so, you know, a definition of intimacy might have to come forth, but they allow themselves individual intimacies with a wide variety of women. They just don't do what I would say ninety-eight percent of lesbian couples do, which is retire. I mean, I've been in this community for a long time and I know when couples break up because they come back out looking for women.

I do think that the structure of the couple is anticommunity. I think that the ways in which they have been able to sustain their relationship is because it is a relationship in community. I've not seen their relationship take precedence over some kind of community endeavor or activity. And I think that's unique. It's absolutely unique. I haven't seen that in any other couple and I've known lots of couples who've been together for years and years and years.

. . . And what I can say in terms of how I differentiate those three entities, the two individual women and the third entity of their relationship, their relationship, i.e., how they, what they stand for together, what their home is that they've built together, what their vision for women is that they've built together, it's always accessible to anyone who's around them.

. . . We share some ideas and ways in which we see, would like to see the world around spiritually, stuff like that, so it's a development between people that I think relationships are about and it's happening with the individual women and then it's also happening with the whole picture, you know, the whole vision. And I feel very comfortable in that.

My experience with most couples in groups is that they are not individuals, that one will speak for the other, depending on who's the more, you know, takes up the more air time. So I never know who I'm dealing with.

But with Chris and Sarah, I know who they are. I know who they individually are. I know who I'm dealing with and they don't speak for each other. They don't expect me to deal with Chris through Sarah or to deal with Sarah through Chris.

In that vein, Chris and Sarah speak of themselves as a couple and how they have built their community, and how each has its place and role.

CHRIS: Last fall, I think maybe it was last fall . . . One of our weekends, work weekends I think it was, there were a lot of women here and we were having a, had a fire out here with the group sitting around and talking and there's another one out by the house there, big fire and they were playing music and everything and this one down here, there was a big, huge political discussion going on. Feminism.

SARAH: It was Memorial Day weekend.

C: It was Memorial Day weekend. . . . We'd been working all day long, I finally, it must have been about 11:30, came up and went to bed. And I woke up, oh, and then before that, Sally . . . had said she was looking for, um, intimates. She was, she was looking for a series of women that she could be intimate with, sort of one-a-month kind of thing. Uh, she didn't want a long-term relationship, she didn't want . . .

S: With one woman.

C: . . . With one woman. She, you know, it's part of all of her politics, but . . .

S: But she missed cuddling and skin-to-skin.

C: Right. Skin-to-skin, that's what I was thinking. And she and Sarah have always been real close and I woke up like at 1:30 in the morning and Sarah wasn't here. Wasn't in bed. And a thought flashed in my mind, "Oh, I wonder if Sarah went off with Sally?" And I was so concerned about it that I went back to bed and went to sleep right away. You know, it was sort of, "I wonder if?" And I mean, it was not something that was going to terribly upset me, I mean, I remember thinking, "Gee, I thought she probably would have discussed it with me first."

S: But she still went to sleep.

C: Yeah.

REFLECTIONS

The women's conversations provide a glimpse into their public and private narratives, and what might cause the differences. Based on the events in each woman's life, the partners decide what will be just for them, what they will share. The couples choose private narratives for sexual intimacy and displays of affection. For some of the couples, this means they do not share these stories with anyone or that they do not touch or kiss if they are not alone. For other couples, this means they will talk briefly of sexual intimacy and they might be physically affectionate with one another. The couples are intensely aware of the limits of a private narrative, and they choose carefully who will know that part of their story. Much of what these women could have shared with friends, acquaintances, and colleagues is lost to the public narrative because the women fear the loss of a job, family connections, and friendships.

Family of origin has a profound influence on how the couples co-construct their public and private narratives. All of the participants are out to their families of origin—their families know they are in a long-term relationship with a woman. Of course, family members react in varying manners. For Sandy and Rita, this means their family members know they are a couple and accept them as a couple. However, the family members do not know the details of their relationship, nor do they see displays of affection between the women. For other couples, sharing this part of their story means their families no longer accept them. Because of the varying reactions, couples can have a public story of what they are and a private story that includes the many other aspects of what being a couple means to them, such as owning a home, having a child, and emotional and physical intimacy.

Rita and Sandy choose to tell their stories and they are allowed to do so. They speak, somewhat in the hope that others will hear and listen. But are there other couples out there sharing their experiences and wisdom? Sandy says she has read "almost everything out there on the subject, but very rarely do you find stories like ours."

These stories can help all of us learn. We can see lessons in the construction of narratives, the impact of the degree to which they are shared. They contain nuggets showing ways to be honest and complete as an individual, how to carry that into a relationship, and how to decide when and with whom to share what they have. Clearly, there are very important people in their lives. How do they sort out who will be most supportive and engage them more deeply?

All of the participants are grateful to be able to share their stories. Sandy and Rita talked about how their participation had an impact on their relationship. In fact, Rita says that this process helped her recognize that "we have couple's stories," and that has brought new meaning and depth to their experience. The women said they felt empowered, and found a renewed feeling and appreciation of their strength as a couple, and in some instances, a renewed appreciation of each other.

⮒ 8   Let's Get Together and Dance

A look at the narratives of all four couples reveals a number of common events and themes that resonate for each couple. Some of these are common to all couples, as the partners begin and continue to build a life together. Some are specific to same-gender couples. All four couples acknowledge that these common events have an impact on their narratives.

In telling of how they got together, all of the couples speak of how they moved "too quickly." Yet, there is not a definition of what "too quickly" might mean. Sandy and Rita speak about the "quickness" with which they found themselves in a couple.

SANDY: I think, at the beginning, it was different for both of us because, well, like a lot of us do, we meet somebody and then, within days or weeks, . . . I've decided that we are a couple and we'll live together forever, and that's kind of how . . . that's where I was coming from even though I didn't know this person. It was like lust at first sight.

I really liked her and I liked her enough that I thought that we probably could become a couple and stay together and it was like that for me almost from the first, second, third time I met her, and it was a lot more sexual at the beginning then, it gradually became, as I got to know her, the real love and respect for her just grew more and more and then I think after we were in therapy and really working on our relationship, that that's when I knew that we, we definitely were going to stay together because we both wanted to stay together and we were both willing to really work on it.

I don't think I was projecting into the future a lot. I mean, I knew that I wanted to just be with her and I thought it was like long term because I really liked her but I wasn't thinking of the future too much at that point. It was, that summer, it was just mostly a week-to-week thing. And, you know, what we were going to do next, we were doing a lot of activities together, we were spending a lot of time together. I didn't really know her and we really weren't talking too much about, I mean, we weren't talking about the future and we weren't, I mean, we didn't know each other so, we were talking about each other and about ourselves and just getting to know each other. So I don't know if I was really, even though I had that feeling that we were going to be together. I don't think we were really talking about it then. Really, the first month or so, I wasn't feeling too much like a couple but it was pretty quick, plus you know how your friends do. Almost from Day One, you're a couple. And they treat you as a couple.

RITA: You know at the party where we met? They were planning our wedding for us.

S: Um hum, they were. They introduced us and . . .

R: Within hours.

S: They were.

R: Friends were.

S: They were real quick, though [laughing].

Quick? Slow? Too fast? Not fast enough? Who has not wrestled with the notion of how soon to take which steps when building a relationship? Sandy and Rita believe their friends might have been quick to treat them like a couple, but they did not actually become a couple for a while.

SANDY: I was more into it right away. We, um, after we met, we went, met one day at a party and within a couple of days, I was thinking of us as a couple. Partly through my history, that's how it had happened for me before and partly because I just, I just really liked her and we seemed to hit if off good, and I was having a really good time and it was very sexual and you know, it was like something that you would never want to end.

And just because lesbians are the way they are, they treat you as a couple right away, so, I was feeling like we were a couple like right away. And I was willing to, I was thinking of it as a long-term relationship right away. I know Rita was coming from a different perspective because of her history.

RITA: Yeah, I was thinking of the moment. I mean, really enjoying being with you. But I wasn't thinking at all, you know, ten years down the road. What I was thinking of was yes, I met you and I really liked you, and I'm very attracted to you, and I'm going back to Colorado, because that's my plan. You know, I had my goals, I had my mission and that wasn't going to change no matter who came into my life. That's how unconnected I was with my feelings and my emotions.

And so, that's what I did. I went back to Colorado after knowing you for almost a year, and I stayed for five months and you flew out. We had done all this before, you know, she flew out a couple times and I flew back once and then, I just knew that, that because you weren't going to come out there because your business had already been established for a year and you were set as far as your business here, you weren't going to change. And, uh, if I wanted to be with you, which I really did, I'd have to move back, so that's what I did.

S: And then I flew out, we drove back together in her car that didn't have a speedometer.

R: That was bad. Having a state trooper come up beside you and you don't know, oh, are you speeding or going too slow.

Can anyone know, except in hindsight, if things built too quickly? Can anyone outside the relationship determine the pace and make a judgment about it? And, why does it matter so? It seems that the speed with which a relationship is built often becomes the focus of blame when a relationship falls apart. That aspect gives women a reason, when there really is no reason, or there are myriad reasons. As with so much in life, the speed of moving into a relationship is relative. Couples might need to negotiate the speed—especially if one prospective partner is accustomed to a much different pace than the other.

As much as pace is important to the women in starting a relationship, it also is important in making major leaps in that relationship, such as Marge and Jill deciding to have a baby.

MARGE: I always thought that, "Oh, it'd be great if you could be a couple and have a house and have a child and or two kids or whatever," but I never thought that was possible. And when I went into the relationship, our story, I never thought it would have that chapter. Personally, for me.

JILL: Yeah. I did after a point, because I came to the point when we'd be out somewhere in the mall or something, and we'd see a baby and I'd be like, "Let's get one of those." But when I entered the relationship, I was twenty-four years old and still, I don't think I entered it going, "OK. Now, I'll be coupled with this person." And, it was like, I guess if I had to describe it, I was learning it.

Because I didn't know where it was going to go or what was going to happen. And I was still dating guys, and you know, I didn't know if this would be something permanent for me or not. And so, I was pretty much taking it day-by-day and seeing where it was going and what was happening and I guess, probably, I'm trying to think of how long we had been together when I realized that this was it and I was going to stay committed to it. Up until that point, I mean, I knew that I loved Marge but I was still kind of confused and not sure, you know, if this is what I wanted and how scary this was going to be to . . . be coupled with someone who, you know, that it was going to be difficult in our culture to do that. And I wasn't sure if I was ready for that and I decided, yes, I was.

M: But that, what was, what was the time span for that?

J: For what?

M: Your deciding, "Well, we'll just wing it," and then, that you were, you are committed.

J: When we moved in together. So, I mean, that wasn't a very long time.

M: Well, it was four or five months. Yeah . . . short time. Then, once I had made that decision, you know, I always saw us, I saw it, that we were going to be together and I don't know how long we had been together when I really started thinking that I wanted to have a baby and I could always see us with a baby, and . . .

Lisa and Elaine haven't placed a judgment on the pace of building their relationship, but they speak in depth about the steps they have taken.

ELAINE: A lot of the time, I'm going, "Oh, I think she'd make a nice friend. She isn't really my type." I got quizzed for three hours one night about my attraction for redheads [laughing]. I had been with a woman who was a ballerina and very feminine.

  And, in the beginning of our relationship, she's walking around all happy and I'm going, "Am I just going along with this because it's easy?" We aren't fighting, and there's no tension here, but I don't know.

LISA: . . . And there was just something about that girl, I think. Maybe I was a little bit disconcerted.

E: Um hmmm. Well, I had a real hard time because I'd been in a relationship for fifteen years with a woman who was bisexual. And it was a hard relationship. Um, I think I was every bit as damaging in it as she was.

  And so I was having a really hard time and I didn't know how hard a time, letting myself be vulnerable, but my former partner and I had just bought a house and we split.

  And then we bought this house and moved in and I literally wouldn't make it mine or take possession of it for about a year and a half. Because I couldn't afford to lose another home. So, I was just kind of poking along and taking my time.

L: And I'm thinking to myself, "Yeah, I know where I am. She'll figure it out eventually. I'm just not going to let it bother me. She'll get there." But after a while, I looked up, I said, "When are you going to make this house yours?"

And that is when Elaine rearranged some of the furniture and actually "moved in" to the house, which was another move into the relationship for her. They also speak of what they carry with them into their relationship.

LISA: I think what I brought to the relationship was I have a very strong sense of honor and a truthfulness and a principle, and absolutely doing the right thing regardless of what it costs you.

ELAINE: Which I had to learn from her.

L: And, I think that I created that in my mind as a child as a survival mechanism of some sort and so I'm really strongly tied to those feelings. And I know that I brought that philosophy to our relationship. I've talked about it a lot. Especially in our early time about what I felt and how important truth is to me. And doing the honorable thing and saying the honorable thing and being, stand up about who and what you were doing.

E: I think what I brought to it was my twins. I've always had somebody because I'm a twin. I went straight from my twin to my first relationship, which went fifteen years. When she met me, it's the first time I've ever been alone. And I'll tell you, going into being alone, I thought I was literally going to die. I think by the time we met, I'd gotten to the point where I was beginning to not only see that it was OK to be alone but beginning to thrive in it. To the point of, I didn't know if I could live with somebody.

But simply the ability to be, to be with someone. In fact, she had some trouble with that because she's more of a loner in some ways. It's like, do you think you could go to another room for a while? Although anymore, it's like I want you in the other room but I want you in my sight. OK, I'll just sit out here, honey. But, yeah, and the intuitiveness that came out of my twin-ness.

L: She's goofy and when she gets a sense of things and a feel of things, it's just uncanny.

Elaine defines one giant step in their relationship—making the house their home.

ELAINE: . . . I thought of the first three or four months we were seeing each other, she'd come visit and stay. Because she was living with her mom, so I couldn't go there.

So, she moved in and I'm compulsive. I know this. And here, I'm walking through my apartment and all of a sudden there's a [soda] can sitting there and there's newspapers here and there and I finally said to her, you know, and she was so brave because she knows how angry I was, I said, "Whatever you need to do to make this place yours," I said, "You can take some responsibility. I wish you would figure that out." And she just looked at me and said, "I have been." OK, I'm married to a slob.

They smile affectionately.

So, when was it that Lisa and Elaine thought of themselves as a couple?

ELAINE: Well, I think after the first weekend.

LISA: Yeah, yeah.

E: That became our first "our story."

L: Yeah, because we started with the story of her just not having, wanting to have anything to do with it. And me having to just chase her all over the place and just pursue it. I mean, that was our first story and we had that from the very beginning. Because I'm going, "I really don't know why it took you so long to make this decision." And, it was humorous to us.

E: The first joke was, it's like I'd spent some time with her and there was a Take Back the Night March, and she and her friends were there, our mutual friends, and I was there and these women were there and I was single, I've never been single and an adult.

And part of me, I mean this is a part of me that's like bravado, I want to try new stuff. These two women had invited me back to their home after the march. And it ended up that I'm walking and all of a sudden she catches up to me. And we spend the whole march, she's asking me all these questions. I'm being interrogated.

L: Oh!

E: And then she invites me to Sarah's for a beer with her and her friends and that's the evening I spent being questioned and maligned.

[Lisa laughs.]

ELAINE: I had an attachment and attraction to redheads, which she now likes and I thought, "I gave up a ménage for this." And that became the joke. But I remember walking away from that . . .

LISA: Probably saved you from diseases.

E: Really!

They both are smiling.

LISA: Not a reputation.

ELAINE: . . . thinking, she's a really nice woman. And I think she'd make a good friend.

L: I mean, she had always liked really feminine women who were either blonde or redheaded. And here I am, I'm not real small and I'm a jock and I'm dark. So . . .

E: Oh, I'll tell the story.

L: What story?

E: This is so evident.

L: [laughing] OK.

E: The first night we're supposed to stay at a friend's house but we lose the bed to another couple, so we go all the way back to my place . . . and, we'd kind of known we were going to spend the night together, so we were each prepared. And somewhere during the evening, we go up to my room and it's like she's on one side of the bed with her back to me, I'm on the other side, we're undressing, we turn to get in bed and we both go . . .

. . . Because I've got on this silky, lacy, baby-blue teddy and she's got on this T-shirt. And, we're both going, "Oh, my! What have I gotten into?"

L: It's true.

E: She's had a lot of luck getting me into T-shirts. Uh, the teddies aren't working.

L: I'm looking at this teddy going, "What the hell do I do with this? . . . How do I get this off?"

E: Yeah, some differences kind of showed up real fast.

L: She didn't throw me out, though.

E: No.

L: So our narrative really started from the very beginning.

E: And we became a "we" very fast.

L: That's true.

E: Really is true, but she didn't have the [truck], she had a little [car], so she had to bring all the pieces.

L: Oh, she was such a goof. I mean, she wants me to be here all the time, but we create the illusion of which I'm not moved in yet. I'm spending every night of the week . . . at some point, I've got to bring more than one suit at a time because it's getting to be a real drag, and she's going, "You haven't moved in yet." And I'm going, "Great." I mean, if you need to create some illusion in your mind, that's fine, but I'm here.

E: I get this, "Oh, well, I've got to leave this suit here because I really need it later, you never know." She wants to move in.

L: [laughing] I'm a really curious person and I ask a lot of questions. Um, especially if I like somebody, I'm intrigued by somebody.

I'm just, exactly what do you think, what do you feel, what do you know, I mean and it's, and I really liked her. I just thought she was really spiffy and she would come up with this generalized, "Oh, you know, I really like redheads." Which baits a lot of questions. At least for me it did. I asked: How did you come to this place and why is that? And so, I was certainly trying to get information about who she was but they weren't interrogations, they weren't severe. More than two hundred questions in an evening. General cross examination.

Elaine was dating four women at the time.

ELAINE: . . . I was living with two friends and the joke was they knew who I was with by who called. I'd come home to like three phone calls and finally, I hadn't been to the ocean in a year. And my first lover and I had a real special place. And I'm looking at the fact that I'm seeing four women.

And I'm writing. I need to go to the ocean and get brown and sit on the beach . . . and figure out what the hell you're doing. It was great, I had women taking me out and giving me gifts that whole week before I left. And, I told them all I would call them when I got back. Well, I already knew before I went that I was going to come back and call her. But, it's like I had to go and do my grieving because I hadn't finished grieving the relationship yet. Do a lot of writing and bought a really tacky shell ashtray for her tacky habit.

LISA: Very tacky.

E: And it was interesting because I drove back and went straight to this one woman's house. And, she's the one I still have great affection for but I think what I needed to do was adopt her.

It's much more a mother-daughter thing, I think. And visited with her and I think pretty much told her that I thought it was going to be pretty serious between Lisa and I. Then the next day, I called another one to tell her and it was kind of a mutual split.

And then I talked to the third one and days were going by. And she's not hearing from me. And it was kind of like I knew I was going to call her, and I made my decision so I wasn't in any rush. I heard about that for years.

Lisa and Elaine share plenty of stories from their early days as a couple that show just how it came about. They include a tale that reminds them that turnabout is fair play.

LISA: Why don't you tell them about Christmas Eve of our first year?

ELAINE: It wasn't my fault. My therapist had heard, I'd come and say, "Well, I think I'm really in love with this woman or that woman," and I'd get this sneer. And I went in and said, "You know, I met this woman the other evening and she's really nice. And I think I'd like her for a friend." Because the other thing I had a hard time with was friendships, I'm real shy. May not be apparent, but I am.

And she said, "Uh, I want to hear more about her." So I told her that she was an attorney. Well, that kind of made her nervous because attorneys, they have big parent ego states. But we started dating and my first partner and I had had a tradition. It's like Ed and Sue were our second family. They were really our good parents. And Sue said, "Why don't you come up Christmas Eve and bring Lisa along. I'd like to meet her." I said, "Cool."

So we get there. They spent the evening interrogating her. I'm just kind of sitting there going, "Oh, god."

L: I'm sitting there going, "Oh, like a guinea pig. OK."

E: Hey, this is mom and dad.

L: Yep, yep. I'm getting all these questions about what I do and how do I feel about power and do I enjoy exercising power and all this and it's like "I love that." So, they were pretty funny. So, that's part of our early narrative. I interrogated her, they interrogated me.

Chris and Sarah also can mark the moment when they first felt themselves as a couple, and it has a link with community.

CHRIS: I suppose when we had that first party. It was like March. That was only about six months after we'd been together. That was pretty soon. We had our first party as a couple. That was important to us. We certainly remember it.

SARAH: We remember the fight more than . . .

C: Right [laughing]. We had our first fight. Well, actually it wasn't our first fight but it was a pretty big one.

S: It was in some way the defining moment.

C: The defining moment, yeah. For years, we wouldn't do carpentry together.

S: [laughing] We still don't.

At least two of the couples were faced with a major change in order to keep the relationship alive. Early on, Elaine insisted that Lisa choose between smoking and being in a relationship with her. Another couple— Marge and Jill—addressed the need for one partner to stop drinking.

ELAINE: Well, I think that we're really, we can really bounce off of each other and take some hard knocks.

LISA: And we both feel very strong, and you know, that's our natural personalities. We're both really feeling-based.

E: I remember about even two or three months in the relationship, she used to smoke. And I sat her down and said, "Look, you know, I will not continue this relationship and number one, I'm terribly allergic and number two, I'm not going to become attached to you and watch you die. And I'm just not even setting myself up for that. So, if you're not going to stop smoking, let me know now." And I must have been pretty selfish . . .

L: . . . My father had died of emphysema and my father and I had a very poor relationship. . . . It was at that point that I realized that it was self-destructive behavior that was attached to my father and my relationship with my father.

E: And then we both gained twenty-five pounds.

Jill and Marge found that their struggle with Marge's drinking came up a few years into their relationship.

JILL: Well, I think it's the fact that I think both of us, I mean we had individual issues that we realized affect us, affected us as a couple, so we both did our own therapeutic processing and knew that we needed to do that in order to have a healthy relationship with each other. And I think had we not made that decision, that there's no way that our relationship would have survived. So I think that going through the process also guided us to where we are and rebuilt or built a healthier coupleship. So I think we each contributed in that way, too.

MARGE: I think we've always made conscious efforts to look towards the relationship. Basically, I suppose one big thing for the relationship was I quit drinking. So that would be part of my work. For the first three years, I drank a lot. It was never to the point where I lost a job or anything, but I am an alcoholic. But then Jill said, "OK, it's either drinking or me," so that was pretty easy.

J: Yeah. I mean she stopped right then and there.

M: Yeah, but I didn't quit smoking until you tried to get pregnant. You said, "I'm trying to get pregnant."

J: Yeah, but that was a decision that you made on your own, really.

REFLECTIONS

It is not unusual that each woman can tell of the moment at which she became aware she was a member of a couple; that each couple can relate that defining moment. They honor that moment in many ways. It is the beginning of a great adventure, the moment they are part of something bigger than themselves, the first step of a journey of a lifetime. These couples regard that moment with happiness, joy, and laughter and recall it as sacred and wonderful, all the while seeing it through the filter of experience and seeing the construction of their past, present, and future narratives.

Getting together, first thinking of themselves as a couple, is a bright and happy memory for all the women. And, almost to a woman, they complain that perhaps they leapt into a relationship a bit too quickly. One couple even brings up the old joke: What does a lesbian take on the second date? A rental truck. Could it be that few lesbians have defined for themselves what a "proper" time span is for beginning a relationship? It would seem that without the heterosexual model of dating, engagement, and marriage, lesbians are left to determine their own models, yet many would prefer to emulate the heterosexual model.

Truly, these four couples are not actively concerned with any heterosexual models, nor do their relationships compare directly. It is here that a few role models might come in handy; it is here that the women might be blazing a trail for others; it is also here that women must determine what is right and true for them, rather than looking outside themselves for some guideline.

⤲ 9   What We Have in Common

There are certain events that occur in any relationship. Among the common themes these couples share are the influences of friends, family of origin, family of choice, therapists and counselors, and work colleagues on the co-construction of their narratives. There are at least two themes that might be expected, but the couples deny experiencing. Much literature has been published on fusion of the partners in a lesbian couple. Among the couples, Chris and Sarah are most vocal in denying it exists in their relationship. Another theme that might be expected is lesbian bed death. The couples who address this subject say their sexual relationships have gone in the opposite direction, that their physical intimacy increases as their relationship grows.

PERHAPS A MYTH

Lesbian bed death is an overused term in the lesbian community. The theory: Once the honeymoon is over, there is a correspondent loss of mutual sexual desire. And, it is believed that this is to be expected. Does it exist? No matter. As long as lesbians believe it exists, it will have an effect. However, the four couples in this study resisted the idea of lesbian bed death. In fact, they are living proof that it is not a given.

Elaine and Lisa speak of the emotional and physical passion they share, which they say is stronger today than when they became a couple.

LISA: So, what do you see for our future?
ELAINE: More and better, I guess. Deeper. I think simpler.

L: Um, hmm.

E: Because at this point, I think we know what's really important to us. We've gotten the sense of our rhythm, and . . .

Jill and Marge learned what all parents learn: The addition of a child means the subtraction of much of what they had become accustomed to as a couple: sleep, time alone, time to focus on one another, money. The joy a child brings to this family cannot be measured. Nor can the amount of work the women face to keep their relationship alive and thriving. While Marge and Jill speak easily of how having a baby has given their relationship more depth, they speak briefly of other, negative effects.

JILL: For me, the only thing it's affected is some of our intimacy and it's just because we're so, both so sleep deprived.

MARGE: Oh, and . . .

J: It seems Friday night . . .

M: Are these supposed to be bad effects?

J: Well, Friday night we always, always used to, we always knew that Friday night we would just be together and rent a movie and just lay on the couch and it just doesn't happen anymore [laughing].

Sarah and Chris note that although the sexual aspect of their relationship isn't the same, it is not the focus of their relationship. They speak of how they draw upon one another for strength, in order to devote more to the women's community.

CHRIS: For me, it's how supportive I am with other women and their lives, and I couldn't do it without the support I have from Sarah. And she, I think with me, if we didn't have each other, we wouldn't be able to have the strength or the resources to do all these other things. But we're not some isolated couple out in suburbia, going off to our jobs, coming home and fixing dinner and watching television and going to bed. So, that's the way our lives work. So, while

I think couple is nice and I'm glad I have it, I think the friendship and commitment to women is really an important thing, as well.

All four couples have a community, but all four give it a unique definition. Marge and Jill have a network of heterosexual and gay and lesbian friends, as do Elaine and Lisa. Rita and Sandy have that network, and include their families of origin.

When they first became couples, the partners tended to focus on one another, putting down the foundations for their relationship. Seeing their photo albums gives a clear picture of this. In their early years, these couples tend to have photos of themselves as a couple, or photos of one partner or the other. As the relationship develops, the women begin spending more time in the community and/or following their individual interests. And, the photo albums show it—they include more and more photos of family and friends.

None of the women shows evidence of the notion of the "fusion of the lesbian couple." Yes, they share interests. Still, these are individuals with tastes, interests, and aspirations that are unique. Their relationships make room for them.

Sandy and Rita talk about shared interests that help build their relationship because they spend time with each other. But in the present, and speculating about the future, they see family and friends playing more significant roles. They speak about what retirement might hold.

RITA: My projects. I certainly haven't thought about yours as much as you have, that's for sure [laughing]. I haven't really talked about what I'm going to do at that time.

SANDY: I guess I just kind of think that because of stuff she's talked about. I think we'll both travel.

R: I hope so.

S: But she likes to travel so much more than I do, so I can envision us traveling together and maybe her traveling also without me.

R: With a friend.

S: Yeah, because she's talked about that. . . . so you think you will do that?

R: I hope so. Yeah, I don't know what else I'll be doing. . . . Maybe it's because I'm enjoying so much what I'm doing right now. I'm not really thinking about retiring, what that's going to be like . . .

S: I think it would be just similar to what you're doing now, maybe just not as much of it, because I'll take over part of it.

R: Well, as far as the projects, but like with the kids, who knows what nieces and nephews are going to have great nieces? . . . I'll always be involved with the children, that's so much fun. And I just don't know what children those are going to be or how many or any of that yet. Camp Rita Day Care.

AND THEN I SAID

All four couples identified at least one person who has had a great influence on the relationship: a therapist, or in some instances, several therapists. The women also cite their friends and family members as influential, but do come back to the roles their therapists have played in the development of their couples' narrative.

CHRIS: We also, in the early years, I'd say the first five years, there were times we did counseling, couples counseling. We had both been in really pretty bad relationships and so we knew what we didn't want it to be like. We didn't always know how to make it like we wanted it and we did a lesbian couples workshop early on that the Gestalt Institute did and we both had done a lot of work with the Gestalt Institute of Cleveland.

SARAH: So we did that, that whole series about body, mind, spirit workshops.

The women had varying experiences with therapy and counselors. Marge and Jill found that individual counseling worked best for them. What they discovered and learned about themselves did have an impact on their relationship. Marge speaks of how becoming moms has affected the couple's intimacy, which she is discussing in therapy.

MARGE: But I never was really a hundred percent efficient in the intimacy aspect anyway and that's why my therapy, I'm going to therapy but I don't know if this has really made it, compounded the problem. Silence is loud as thunder.

Sandy and Rita also believe that individual counseling can have a positive effect on their relationship, and they are committed to taking it another step—couples counseling.

SANDY: I've read that as women get older, they become more introspective. That's why I thought it might be partly age, but I think for me probably the most important thing is being in therapy because I'm so active and so busy . . . before therapy I never took time to sit down and really think about my feelings and going to therapy, that forces me to sit down and, you know, when they ask these questions, you have to sit down and think about the answers.

It's like, "Uh, I don't know about that one. I have to think about it," because I've never thought about it before. And so, being in therapy and I'm in group therapy also, it's all about feelings, so you have to think about your feelings, get in touch with your feelings, being able to verbalize what you're feeling . . . own your feelings.

All that stuff, and so I've learned to do that. I never did that before. There was an "ah, ha!" though, once. Right at the beginning of therapy. . . . I remember not even hardly realizing I had an inner life, a feeling life. I was sweeping the house one day. I was sweeping with a sweeper and it was like I was thinking about something. It was like, "Oh, wow! This is like there's another me in here." It was really weird. It was like, "ha!" You know, it was a strange feeling because it wasn't all out there and I guess I'd never even realized I had an "in here" before. So, I remember that being a really different kind of feeling. Like a realization thing.

In another part of the conversation, Sandy and Rita address therapy again.

SANDY: . . . That's a big reason that I stay in therapy because I think the more I know myself, the better partner I can be, because then I can let her know who I am, too. And how can I let her know if I don't know? And, I have a lot of trouble with conflict, so that's what we're working on right now. I just do not like conflict at all. I run from it, so I'm working on that.

RITA: I have a problem with anger, so we have this vicious cycle that occurs with heated topics, and that is, I'll have anger and then you're . . .

S: I hide.

R: Yeah.

S: Because I don't want to deal with it.

R: And then the conversation won't be . . . and so there isn't really any resolution, which is something that we're going back to joint counseling sometime in the next month or two. We'll have a couple, few sessions and learn how to do that. Which we've done all through the relationship.

You know, we started each, and together we started after five years in the relationship. We went together and then we continued individually, so I've been, you know, over seven years individually. And we've gone, this would be probably the third time as a couple that we'll go back. And just, no crises in the relationship but just to make tune-ups.

S: To get some professional help.

R: . . . You know, with some things. Tune-ups and, just, I think for me a better picture of what I'm doing. You know, because sometimes it's hard to see it without someone else besides, well, other than Sandy.

S: Yeah, objective.

R: Objective. Yeah.

S: Yeah. It's always worked well for us. Some couples, I think can do it with friends but I don't know. It's never seemed to work out for us with the therapy that really focuses on what you want to be doing. I mean, you just can't chit chat. They tend to bring you back to the subject.

It takes little imagination to see that counseling is a linchpin for Lisa and Elaine's relationship—they see counselors individually and to-gether— Elaine is a therapist.

LISA: The level of our connection . . . we've worked at our relationship. We've done a lot of therapy, separately and together, and I can't imagine ever being able to re-create that with anybody else.

Lisa and Elaine have learned how to fight cleanly, without trying to deliberately hurt the other, how to build a relationship, and how the past has had a distinct influence on their stories.

LISA: . . . Elaine and I were both severely abused as children. And so, we've had a lot of ground to cover. And, there are just things that when you've been abused that you get kicked off in relationships . . . it just happens. And we've both worked really, really hard on our abuse issues.

We've done a lot of individual therapy and each of us has gone through really bleak times personally during our relationship. Pe-riods of time when we couldn't be comfortable being sexual with each other because it was just too mishmashed with the past. Times when one of us has had incredible anger going and we've taken turns with that and we've hit periods of rage.

I think we sort of cleverly never quite do that at the same time and so it's her turn and then it's my turn and then it's her turn. And we've sort of worked through and my sense is that we're both right about now beginning to pop out the end of that tunnel. In the sense that she's feeling really good, I'm beginning to feel really good . . . where there's a little congruence in my feelings and I can feel a full spectrum and so can she.

CELEBRATING OUR RELATIONSHIPS

No matter what the conditions of their families, these women grew up seeing, and learning to believe, that American life revolves around family and friends. So, what to do when that same America does not recognize or condone same-gender marriages?

Each couple has a ceremony or ritual to celebrate the relationship and to make a formal commitment, one of many rituals that can add support and structure to a relationship. Sandy and Rita describe a ceremony that reflects what they know "wedding ceremonies to be like."

RITA: It was real important for me then to have that holy union, which we had after two years and three months together, on August 25, 1985. We had a holy union.

SANDY: At what time?

R: Well, is it, what time was that? I don't remember . . .

S: In the morning . . . we had the reception, the cake. We did that, we cut each other's, and you know, fed each other . . .

R: Oh, a gaggy thing that you see the heterosexual world do.

S: But I *had* to do it to feel committed.

R: We asked our families if they'd be involved. And my brother, John, who's four years younger, he's the one whose boy I baby-sit for, and the little girl. I'm real close with him. He's a singer and he sang and it was just beautiful. Another mutual friend, Jenny, came and tape-recorded it for us. We sit and listen to that prayer that we wrote together and the whole thing. Which is fun. It's kind of fun looking through pictures and looking back on . . .

S: Home movies.

Chris and Sarah speak of a more nontraditional ceremony.

CHRIS: Since we both were in relationships before that were nine years long . . . both of us wanted to give ourselves a good bit after nine years to where we were really able to sort of celebrate our relationship. We had sort of a celebration and we've been together twelve years. And nine years was, for us, rather pivotal. We both had put up with a lot from other relationships. This one is very different.

SARAH: It has been.

C: We had a group of about twenty close women down here. And those were close friends to good friends and it started on Saturday morning and ran all the way to Sunday afternoon.

S: We had asked a friend of ours, the person that we both talk to, to plan it and she pulled in each woman that was there and what they meant, what we meant to their lives. She pulled in the ancestors and they made banners for us that are hanging in the pool room . . . uh, the past, the present, and the future.

C: It was a big celebration, lots of food, people enjoying themselves and we even had a swimming pool ritual.

Later, Chris and Sarah talk about what sort of ritual that was.

SARAH: There was light floating on the water, just candled, which is sort of supernatural anyhow. And then all these women in their birthday suits without all the trappings, that we see the pureness of that, that we all start nude and naked, much like a newborn baby and yet, there's a ritual and a celebration in that about that, that starting and we have to make it happen.

At different points in our lives to remember who we are, why we are here. And it's also remembering that life is fun and play.

The couples also speak of how important it is to recognize their anniversaries. Sandy and Rita find a special purpose in this.

RITA: It's a remembering. It's not necessarily a recommitment but it's just good for me to listen to [the audio tape of their ceremony].

SANDY: Do you think maybe it is a recommitment? That's kind of how, even though I didn't need it at the time, I think that kind of is a recommitment in a way from just listening to it. I mean, I always feel really close to you when we listen to it together.

These commitment ceremonies are not sanctioned, legally or socially, but all the couples talk about anniversary dates. They choose to celebrate the date they became a couple and the date of their commitment ceremony, and, for Chris and Sarah, the date of proving to themselves that they indeed had become a couple and that there were signs that they would continue as one. The commitment ceremony also gives the couples a chance to make their relationship public to friends and members of their families.

REFLECTIONS

There are major life transitions that affect the couples' narratives, such as getting a job, changing careers, retiring, or having a child. None of these women has walked away from the challenge. Once they formed these relationships, they did not stop and rest. They have realized they must know what their relationship is and put in effort to make it what they want. A common theme in these couples' narratives is the influence of significant persons in their lives. All the couples have been through crises that have required love, strength, stability, and focus. What sustains these couples when they are troubled? Who can they call upon—themselves? Their partner? Friends? Family? All four couples said therapists—individual, couples, and/or group—have significant impact on the couples' narrative, as do friends, family of origin, family of choice, and community. There are sounding boards and listeners and mirrors. Some work, some don't. Are the women resilient enough to keep trying?

Working with the women, individually and within their community, reveals quite clearly that there are more than two people in these relationships. The relationship, always in the midst of being defined and redefined, created and re-created, has a life of its own. And there are individuals, groups, and community to support the relationships.

All of the women talk about the importance of working on their relationship; and they seem to be surprised by the amount of work it takes. The women also have an awareness of their relationship, a perspective of it as an entity separate from themselves, a living and breathing and dreaming life-form, which they can and do construct.

Sarah and Chris speak extensively of their roles in the women's community, in particular the lesbian community. Elaine and Lisa and Jill and Marge speak of how friends have important places in their lives. Rita and Sandy talk of their relationships with their families of origin, especially with their nieces and nephews. Sandy and Rita also point to the importance of friends and other couples who not only support them, but become role models. All the couples, regardless of how out they are, speak of how important it is to immerse themselves in the lesbian community, even if just for fleeting moments. It is such immersion that helps sustain their relationships.

The women all have ways to mark milestones in their life as a couple. Some choose to be more public, but all make it a point to mark the passages. What is it about these ceremonies that support and strengthen their sense of being a couple?

There are other bonds that strengthen, including setting goals, starting a family, taking in family, developing circles of friends, and building a community. All of these contribute to the reality and solidity of the relationship. The women recognize the need for such bonds. How do they choose them? How do they sustain and strengthen them?

Some experiences are unique to one couple, and the effects have proved to be profound.

Two serious accidents forced many changes in Rita's life. Rita and Sandy do not speak of the accidents much now; they happened several years ago. They both live with the consequences. It is Sandy's sister who first brings up the subject, while she speaks of how each brings a positive outlook into their relationship.

SISTER: I would say so, um, Rita a lot. I've seen her struggle through a lot and she always, always can find the good in everything. She's just one of these people that'll always look for the good rather than the bad. Not that [Sandy] is a negative but Rita's more of an outstanding positive. I mean, just seeing what she's gone through and how her life has changed.

Sandy's sister added that in spite of the auto accidents and the continuing problems, Rita's "just fun to be around." When asked about it, Sandy and Rita speak in detail about the accidents and how they changed their narrative, specifically ending Rita's distance running and generally slowing her down. They view the changes as positive, though she lives with chronic pain. And Sandy tells of how angry Rita was for a long time, but that "gradually she resolved it somehow. And doesn't talk about it much at all."

The two car accidents, in which Rita was rear-ended each time, happened in a four-month span. She tells of the major changes they forced in her life, and, as a result, in their couples' story.

RITA: That really changed my life. It was September 5, 1985, was the first accident. I was rear-ended. And that caused significant damage to my body, my neck and my back. Then, four months after that, I had my second rear-end accident, on January 5 of 1986. So it's been over ten years . . . but I went through about three years of rehabilitation.

I used to be a marathon runner, track . . . and then I couldn't do those activities. I'm really happy that I can walk and ride my bicycle and those are the activities that I learned are OK for my body and work well for my body. Changed me and it changed our relationship because I wasn't running, running, running.

Yeah, I mean good things came out of it. I was able to slow down, look at myself and start doing that introspective stuff . . . that we were talking about you having, not needing an accident to do, but that's what happened.

It's still chronic. It's chronic pain. And I do the exercises every day. I've gone through different phases as far as communicating about it and all that. I talked a lot about it the first five years. So much so that I don't know if I'll ever talk about it again. [She laughs.] That's kind of why, it's just a part of my life now that doesn't seem necessary for me to talk about. But it sure did change my life. It did definitely change our story.

SANDY: She was real, well, I don't know if you know many marathon runners, but they're a little obsessive with the running and she was pretty obsessive and it didn't matter what kind of plans you had when it had to revolve around the running schedule.

R: I'd run every day.

S: Yeah.

R: Eighty miles a week, so . . .

S: So, when she quit running, it gave us more time together. And it slowed her way down. And she went through some bad times, I mean, because when she was having real bad pain, we had to rent a hospital bed and I don't think you had any insurance at that time, so we rented a hospital bed, put it in the living room, and hired one of our friends to stay with her because she couldn't move, had to be helped back and forth to the bathroom.

She was real angry about it for a while. A long time. And we had to talk about it. But then gradually she resolved it somehow. And doesn't talk about it much at all. Which is OK now because she doesn't need to.

But, yeah, that changed a lot of stuff and a lot of positives came out of it even though she ended up with the chronic pain. A lot of positives.

Marge and Jill already have discussed their life-changing event—their daughter's birth—and how it has affected them and their relationships.

Chris and Sarah have a unique approach to community among these couples. They also have a child in their lives, by way of taking in Sarah's niece when she was pregnant. The effect the boy has had on them surfaces happily while they go through their photos.

SARAH: Well, when my niece came, she came to say she was having a baby, which we're having a baby. So, that meant the child in our lives.

As they look over their photos, there are plenty of Jeffrey. Chris points out a photo of when he was born. Later a photo of their house.

CHRIS: Well, it was when Jeffrey was a baby.

SARAH: And, uh, we stayed in tents. Then we had the cabin built.

C: Want to make a kid happy, give him a really big cardboard box.

S: . . . This is Chris's parents. And the rest of my family. It's Chris's birthday, obviously. That's Jeffrey. Such a happy baby. I'm giving him a bath. This is his mom.

Later they speak of Chris's dad putting up a swing for Jeffrey.

SARAH: . . . And helping us build our fence for the goats. Swimming pool. We're picking red raspberries, that's up here. Christmas. Our first Christmas in the house.

CHRIS: It was exciting, of course. You build your house, your dream.

S: And we have a tent up in the living room.

C: Jeffrey. It's a Jeffrey thing.

S: Snowmobile. Taking them to [Florida]. . . . And the campfire.

C: Obviously, Jeffrey's been a big part of our life the last fourteen years. OK, more Miss P and Jeffrey. More Jeffrey. More and more Jeffrey. Jeffrey and his mother. He saw all these pictures when he was down here, didn't he? He was here for his break in school. . . . You know, these early years are, we were much more diversified in terms of, we were much more involved with family, I think, and less involved in the women's community. You can see how that gradually changes.

Here we are [in Florida]. We went down there.

Well, people grow up, you know, kids grow up and they don't need you as much. And our relationship's changed with that, I think. We served a real purpose when Sarah's family, uh, sister's children were young and she had greater financial need . . .

S: She was divorced.

C: So we helped out a lot. Sarah before me and then the two of us. But that's changed now. They're grown up.

And, so they started developing their vision of the women's community. Before they opened their bed and breakfast, they had an exchange program of sorts, for two summers hosting women from Japan and the Soviet Union, the result of belonging to a peace group.

Chris and Sarah made a conscious choice to take advantage of one thing that is seemingly eternal and eternally changing.

SARAH: The land, the actual physical land nourishes me. Having the access to hear the birds sing without sirens in the background. Looking out our window when we get up in the morning and seeing deer in the field, playing in the soil, looking at a hillside and down the hills. They nourish me.

CHRIS: Keep you going. And I think when we were up in [the city] yes, we were involved some in the women's community, but we were pretty much into ourselves and that was early into our relationship, too, so, I think you're always, usually into more your-selves in the early part of a relationship, anyway. So, that was up there and by the time we were down here, we were sort of reaching out more.

S: But I think that all relationships do that, even in the heterosexual, for that time. It's just the two of them and they branch out in different ways. They have kids, they get in school activities or whatever, but, I think if you don't do that, you're expecting that other person in this couplehood to meet all your needs.

And you soon learn about them enough to know that they can't do that. Even if that was, even if they wanted to, they can't physically do that. So, if you're going to have your needs met, you have to reach out.

They point out the parallels between being on the land and their relationship.

CHRIS: I think, Sarah, your experience as an African-American has been a part of it.

SARAH: The concept of a village is very much a concept I believe in. I think society has lost a lot of it in the process. The other part is our whole belief in the Mother Earth and we need to respect this land and give to this land.

Sailing can be seen somewhat as a metaphor for the relationship between Elaine and Lisa. Their skills and knowledge of sailing have grown just as their relationship has grown. They have taken risks and seen that things can work out, they hit stormy seas and work together to find smooth water again.

LISA: We don't really fight very often.

ELAINE: We fight on the boat. I call her the Apparent Captain. She's very, she's an athlete. She's a natural athlete and I am not. And being dyslexic doesn't help that. So, she usually manages the helm and I like to crew and I do that. But I've got all the book learning because I'm passionate about sailing so I take the classes. I know the rules, so she holds the wheel. And I call her the Apparent Captain.

And I just say, you know, "Some things, if I tell you do something, do it." And then we'll talk about it. It's like this big freighter was coming through and blew his horn one time and I knew that meant that we needed to get to starboard real fast. It was like, "Move that way." It's like, "Just move it." The other thing we do, is we bought a little boat first. And I had to learn starboard and port. I cannot do left and right. And I told her, I will not move if you say left and right because I'm going to do something wrong. So we're out sailing one day, she's at the helm and she told me to do something to the right and I just sat there and it's like I didn't want to sit there but I'm just sitting and she finally came up with starboard.

L: If I'm afraid I don't stay scared, I go to anger from it. And, in some instances, that's a really good thing and in others . . .

E: It's not a very pleasant thing to watch her.

L: I mean, we would do that a fair amount and, my favorite boat story is when we first got this boat. I mean, you talk about a couple of idiots. We buy this twelve-and-a-half-foot boat.

E: On vacation.

L: On vacation.

E: Impulse.

L: OK. We have never sailed in our lives. We are on a barrier island, so we're sailing between the mainland and this barrier island. All right. But you know the ocean's out there. It's not that far away. And there are tides and all kinds of stuff.

E: May I interject something? I almost died in a white-water rafting accident.

L: Yeah. So we have one sailing lesson on this area and we decide we're going to sail. The only thing he told us was if you see white caps, don't go out. Well, we don't and it's windy.

E: No white caps, though.

L: We didn't see any white caps. So we decide we'll go sail out there. And we have no motor. And this area we're going out in has these pylons and then there's a little tiny exit and entrance. Well, we get out there and we're sailing.

E: I mean, the wind takes us.

L: Yeah, and it's like, well the white caps were all going in that direction, so we couldn't see them.

E: From the shore.

L: It's like, Jesus!

E: But I mean we sailed that boat like we'd been sailing for years. We just turned it around and did it. And then the next time we went out, we grounded ourselves, and I thought you were going to tell the story.

L: Yeah, she got scared and she disappeared on me.

E: I froze.

L: She froze and I'm sailing this boat by myself and I'm going, "Elaine, Elaine, Elaine." She's gone and I ended up putting it on the ground. And I'm mad because I'm scared and what's even worse is, I hate snakes, and we're on marsh grass. And somebody has got to get out of this boat and push this boat off and I'm sitting there thinking salt water, salt water, are there snakes in salt water? I'm trying to figure this out because I mean, if there's snakes . . . I will just die. Well, I decided there weren't. So I jump off the side and push us off.

E: And we sailed to shore. And we walk up to this picnic table and she says, "I don't care what you have to do to get over this but you better do it now." And, I've never frozen before, that I knew. And I sat there for about two minutes and I don't remember what I thought. I don't know that I thought anything, but I got up and from then on we were fine. It was the first time I'd felt in danger on water, I think, since that accident.

L: But those are the worst fights we've had, they are on our boat. I mean, we have disagreements but we just sort of talk about it, I mean we just don't get to a point where, it's like I don't want to irritate her. And she doesn't want to irritate me and we don't work at trying to mess with each other. It's like, OK, we have a problem here. What's the issue, what do we need to get it solved?

E: To the point that we dock so well now that people applaud.

L: It's like last year, for example. This could have been an ugly inci-
dent, I mean, we were doing something on the boat and I was upset
because there was just something happening and I wasn't sure we
were going to be able to do what we needed to do and I was scared
and I was angry, and when I'm angry, I don't exactly direct it at her,
it's just like all these expletives that are sort of going into the uni-
verse.

And she didn't say anything and we got it docked and we went
in and had dinner. And we're sitting and eating dinner and she
looks at me and she says, "You know, your abusiveness on the boat
is absolutely unacceptable to me. I can't do this anymore. I don't
know what you need to do but this is really harmful and it hurts me
and I don't want to be treated like this."

Well, I felt this big. I mean, I apologized and I haven't done it
since and it's like any time I want to say anything and I just sort of
bite my shirt and it's that kind of stuff.

E: Well, that comes from knowing each other, too. Because I know
that when she gets really scared she goes to rage. And I knew she
was scared so I just kind of held my tongue and I got it handled.
But I was still angry and I'm going, "OK." My therapists keep telling me this and I tell this to my clients, so it must be true, you need
to shift the discomfort back to where it belongs.

And she hasn't killed me yet, so, at that point, I just said, "Look,
this is not acceptable to me. Whatever you need to do, do it." And
then there was this silence and I know her well enough to know
that she's honorable and she'll think about it and get back to me.

But there's this silence and I'm going, "Oh shit! Oh shit! Oh
shit! She's really pissed now. I wish I hadn't done that." I was still
uncomfortable.

But, about ten minutes later, she said, "OK, this is what was going on and this is what I'll do from now on." I said, "Fine, that's
great." And so, she did. The next time she said, "I'm starting to get
scared." It's like, OK, I think when you're on a big lake on a boat
and we know what we were doing . . . life and death, it just gets real
clear.

L: . . . We're good out there. But it's like the waves are big and it's scary sometimes and the wind and trying to dock that boat . . . You've got to know what you're doing. But we got there.

REFLECTIONS

These events and stories remind us that each couple is unique. Each couple has different influences, lives in a circle all its own, and the women bring different experiences to the relationship. And, no matter how similar couples might appear, all these differences send the women on differing paths. The common themes and common experiences will occur, yet the relationship will be heavily influenced by events, from mundane to life-changing, that are unique to that couple, to those women.

How have these women remained flexible in meeting the unexpected? It might be that the foundations of their relationships have been strong enough to weather these storms, and allow the women to maintain a bend-but-don't-break attitude in the most desperate of times.

➢ 11   Five Years Later

These women continue their relationships, learning, developing and adding threads to their already wonderfully colorful stories. We have listened to their stories on how their relationships started and the many, many ways in which they have grown. They, and we, remain in the middle of the stories, not knowing how they might end.

Five years after the first conversations, another visit with the women provided a chance to catch up on their lives and relationships. The passage of time and scheduling problems take a toll. One couple, Marge and Jill, are not included in this section.

SANDY AND RITA

Sandy and Rita have made material changes—they sold the cabin and their boat. And they added a black Labrador puppy to their family.

SANDY: We're a little bit older and, hopefully, a little bit wiser. I don't know.

RITA: A lot wiser.

S: We are wiser. . . . One of the most significant things that has happened to me in the last couple years is, about a year ago I met a woman. She's a psychic and a spiritual shaman. And I've been really intrigued with her and have really got into spirituality, not into any particular religion as such, but just spirituality and I think it's really starting to change me, to soften me up, to make me a more loving person. I'm taking a little bit more time for myself this year.

Later, she picks up the theme.

SANDY: I was in counseling for years. I did ten years of individual counseling. That's ended. And I did four years of group counseling, once a week for four years and I took a couple summers off, but that's ended. I think I've really progressed and I ended on a very good note.

I don't think it's my way anymore. I think the spirituality is really, really helping me. The main reason I was in counseling for all that time was because of being sexually abused by my grandfather and now, although I said I would never do this—it's a complete change for me—I'm working on forgiving him and I think I'm almost there.

It's not even just him, it's a whole forgiveness of the human race type thing. And, it's really, really helpful.

Rita also spoke of turning inward.

RITA: I began taking Tai Chi. It's a slow movement meditation course. It's been really good for me in a lot of ways. It's, I think, helped me to relax more. It's another way to start my day after I do my twenty-minute transcendental meditation and then I go into the living room and do some warm-up exercises and do a little bit of my Tai Chi form.

My instructor is a very gentle, loving man and it's been really good for me to get to know him and to share things with him and the other two or three or four individuals in the class. I also ended my individual counseling. So that had been almost ten years that I had been in individual counseling, so that's been a transition for me. I thought it was time for me to move on, just move in a different direction, so that's what I've done.

And I am learning to forgive. I have a ways to go with that but I am learning to forgive. I think that I'm learning to be even more grateful for those things in my life daily that I look around and see and notice and am grateful . . . for so many things. I think I'm just in a different direction. Like Sandy, I'm growing more spiritually and that seems to be the path that I'll be taking.

Rita and Sandy sold their cottage and the boat so they would have more free time. And they have spent that time with Mattie, puppy-proofing the house, going to obedience classes, and romping, as any black Lab would want.

The time they have freed also allows them to enjoy children.

RITA: . . . The nieces and nephews. They're a huge part of our lives. We have eighteen nieces and nephews between us and, as you know, I've spent lots of time with Cody. He's now my six-year-old nephew and he has a little sister Casey and she's now three and a half.

Again, I cannot tell you how much these children have brought to my life. The joy, the happiness, the child in me coming out. It's just been so wonderful helping to raise them, to love them, and to spend so much quality time with them.

Now, between us, we have four nieces and nephews that this year are graduating from high school. So right now we're in the midst of graduations and graduation parties and each of these children, young adults, are heading to college and we're very involved with where they're going and I'm sure we'll visit each of them.

Although we can't say enough about how much we love them, it really is time consuming and our calendar is booked and booked and booked with events with the children.

After talking about what changes they had made individually, Rita and Sandy spoke of their relationship, how they have changed and grown together, and how their individual changes have affected the relationship.

RITA: We just celebrated our sixteenth anniversary. I think more important than that is not the years but the quality of our relationship. I can't say enough about how each of us are so committed to our individual growth, to the growth with various friends and especially committed to our relationship to each other to wanting to spend time together, to looking forward to seeing each other every day, to hearing about each other's day, to laughing together, to just really truly deeply enjoying each other's company and I don't know a lot of couples that can say that and I'm just so grateful and so thankful to have you in my life. Again and again I'm blessed.

SANDY: I feel the same. We've always been close but it seems like every year we get a little closer and whenever we do anything individually, especially working on ourselves, that just makes us closer and our relationship more intimate. We're just able to open up more, our inner selves, and show it to each other. And we're very supportive too.

We have our anger things and we still have our little fights, but I think they're fewer. And I think that they're a lot shorter time. I think we're more forgiving of each other. And I know Rita is definitely less angry than she used to be. A lot less angry. So, I'm really grateful for that.

R: So am I. It's nice not to be in that space so much. To be more gentle and to be more loving and to be more compassionate and if, because I'm not so angry that I have the opportunity to be more gentle and am.

As for the intimacy in their relationship . . .

SANDY: There's a difference between intimacy and sex, so it's hard to know which one to talk about. We've always been sexually active. I think that's very important. A very important way of staying close and it's really involved with intimacy. It's hard to separate them, although you can be very intimate without sex. It's nice to be intimate with sex, too.

RITA: I think it's interesting to think about our relationship and the intimacy that we shared, let's say, during the first five years, because I thought that that was like really deep, really cool, like the best.

And then, between years five and ten, we seemed to not have as much sex and yet I felt even closer to you, a deeper sense of closeness. And thinking, it can't get any better than this. And now, between ten and sixteen years, I'm thinking, this is just excellent! Our relationship is just getting deeper and deeper and more loving and more loving, and of course, like any relationship, we've had our roller coaster. We've had our ups and downs and we'll continue to have our problems and work them out.

It's hard to describe the deepness of the love. It keeps growing and growing and growing. So I can't imagine what it's going to be like in another sixteen years.

S: And we're grateful for each other and we're both very verbal about thanking each other and being grateful to each other, respecting each other. I think that's really important. We see so many couples that don't respect each other and I think that's real important and I think it's real important to talk about it, too.

Finally, they mused on what it was like to share their stories, to open their relationship to questioning and scrutiny.

SANDY: I think that it's great that other people have found it helpful, by what we said. It's always nice to be helpful.

RITA: I feel good that I can be helpful and it's nice to know that other people reading or knowing about our relationship can help them in any way. There's only good that can come from that.

S: Yeah.

CHRIS AND SARAH

Chris and Sarah also had some major changes in their lives. They remain together, part of their community, and devoted to the land.

CHRIS: I think that we've had a fair amount of illness. Jane, our other housemate, had a quintuple bypass, and during the same period, Sarah had two very mild strokes.

And so, we had some real issues around fear and fear of how we're going to move along and I had fears about Sarah and Jane being alone at the farm and they've had fears about their own health status and part of that resulted in probably some ill-thought-out movement towards getting, having some other women live at the farm. We actually built them a small cabin and made plans for them to come and live and they did for nearly two years. And that subsequently didn't work out.

I think we learned a lot about ourselves in that whole process around some of the issues of living with other people and having common values, which became a really important theme. Because if we don't have those common values, it's hard to work out the other stuff.

We've also had another woman come live at our place permanently. She actually built a house on our land and she shares most meals with us. Her name is Millie and she is very handy. . . . She was in a long-term relationship with someone who died.

. . . I think we're all learning to communicate better around a lot of issues.

SARAH: To elaborate a little bit more on the impact of illness, what illness did to me specifically at the time that I had my strokes, was it made me realize my whole mortality and that all we're promised are moments. And, coming to terms with that, that you need to create what you want at the moment that you have because that's all you have.

And so the process of these last few years has been not just believing that as a concept but believing it as a reality and then living it and knowing it.

The other thing regarding health that's impacted me is that I'm the caregiver for Jane. And giving care to someone that can no longer function as an independent person and needs someone around . . . has made me realize that you lose part of your freedom in that process . . . and adjusting to that and how you claim back some of that freedom and still have time for yourself so that you have time to grow, and have time for us as a couple so we have time to grow, and have time to do the other things that you believe in, in life.

So those basically have taken up a lot of time. In the process, I have learned to be more disciplined most of the time about writing.

I do write more. I share those writings with other people but still my writings are very personal and that's what they're remaining at the moment.

Chris was preparing for retirement, after twenty-two years at a university. She also was taking a trip to Eastern Europe, noting it would be the first time in their twenty-two years as a couple that she had gone on a trip of any duration without Sarah. Chris and Sarah knew they were moving into a new phase of life, and knew that they had no clear vision of the shape it would take. They were confident they would shape the new aspects of their lives just as they had in the past.

CHRIS: In terms of being a couple, I think we're at least as solid a couple as before. Nothing's happened to weaken that. If anything, perhaps we're a little more solid or I'm more solid with it.

And I'm not really meaning to say that we, that I wasn't solid with it before. Sarah and I were just talking . . . and I think just the fact that I do feel more comfortable sort of testing out my aloneness stuff and realizing that that's something that's important to me and that I want to investigate and invest in. In our relationship, I think we both always have taken pride in the fact that we're two separate people and that we're a couple, as well. But that separateness, I guess I want to define it a little more and for me right now, it seems a good way to define that is to be off doing something on my own.

SARAH: I think, how I see us, it's not to do with we're solid or not. It's in a way I see us as more expanded as to who we are, in that part of that allows for a greater experience to come into that. One is this time away from each other, that Chris can do all the things she likes and I can be secure that whatever that perimeter takes, that does not diminish that she loves me and that who I am as a person is still as valuable and who we are as a relationship is still as valuable to her as it was before. . . . That she's still very much a part of me and still a part of this couple.

C: I think some of your searching this way in terms of your self, has been doing it more introspectively in terms of your writing and I've not done that . . . I might do that someday, but it's not where I am right now, so my globetrotting, my investigating the world, shall we say, is part of what I'm thinking is going to help me find out who I am, what I'm interested in. And it adds sort of an excitement that I think will be very interesting and I think it will be very interesting to our relationship to have added that.

S: Right. And just like my writing does as we share that, that piece of what I do, I think it enriches our relationship. And I think this experience of yours will enrich our relationship too.

The women agree that as they grow older, they can see their relationship growing deeper. They have developed an intimacy that buoys them even though, with Sarah as a caregiver, they must plan carefully to have time alone and time together. They are aware they need to work in more time for fun, but they are comfortable.

CHRIS: I think sex has always been an issue in our relationship. It's something that's very difficult for me. I've never really worked through some of the issues around sex and [not] feeling very comfortable with either talking about it or doing it.

I can't say that we've really totally experienced lesbian bed death, although sex is not something that for me has ever been of major importance. Well, maybe back in my twenties it was a big focus or early thirties. I think that changed even more when I had a hysterectomy in my early forties. I don't know. I think it gave me another excuse or something. A sexual relationship is something that we continue, but it's not something that we focus on a lot.

I think we've done some transitioning around it, come to terms with it. Where we're at is OK with me most of the time.

SARAH: I delved recently in some writings . . . I said that one of the fears that I had was the fear of being alone and having people not like me.

Growing up, there were a lot of reasons that I didn't perceive myself as being liked, and all those reasons were justified from the society around me. But one of the things that people liked about me is that I had a nice sexual body. And so, I felt sex, if you wanted people to like you, you had to have, use your, let them have sex.

And so sex, having where Chris came from and my sexual needs and trying to look at them in that way, being afraid she'd leave if I didn't have sex with her ended up being a conflict. . . . and, taking high doses of blood-pressure medicine decreases your sexual needs, decreased my sexual desires. . . . We've met in a middle ground and maybe we're not always going to be comfortable with where we're at, but I think we're both comfortable with where we're at, at the moment.

And I know that's probably the last reason she'll leave me is because I don't give her, give her sex, and so I don't have to worry about her leaving me for that reason.

C: That's interesting. . . . You still think about my leaving you. You know, it's just never something I ever think about is your leaving me or my leaving you.

LISA AND ELAINE

This couple, too, has seen many changes, some major, and their life together is going well.

ELAINE: Well, I was just thinking about how many changes we've gone through and how many things we've been through. We went through another campaign. And, this time, we decided to do it openly. I think it was an open secret anyway. It was too hard on us to not do it anymore and I think Lisa, in particular, decided that regardless of if she won or lost we wouldn't have to deal with it anymore. I mean, it was so much better doing it open because I got a lot of support, which I didn't have before, and that helped us.

LISA: I think that what happened for me is that they were saying it about me anyway. OK. And I was hearing it anyway. . . . I mean, it's like there's all this power over me if I twitch about it.

And so I just sort of took the attitude: OK, so? And your point is? I just sort of went about my life the way I normally go about my life and what I found is that people around me were so incensed by what [the campaign opponents] were attempting to do to me that it was very empowering to see all these people really resentful of that being done to somebody who they consider to be a decent human being.

E: We thought about it as like being in the closet with the door open. It's like we weren't necessarily out there telling everybody but I found that we were together a lot. We were using couples' language . . . it's hard not to at this point.

L: . . . And I went to some friends and said: Will you do a fund-raiser for me? Let's just ask everybody in the community and have a big party. I mean, if I've got the name, I might as well get the benefits of it . . .

We had this party and there must have been a hundred people there. I mean, it was a huge success. People had a good time and people got involved in the process. And so, what potentially could have been a detriment actually turned out to be a very positive thing, you know, from a political perspective.

And there was a positive result, from an individual perspective. During the campaign, Elaine met several people, including three women who put in a great deal of time on the campaign and who remain friends with Lisa and Elaine.

LISA: You know, in our relationship, I would never want to be experiencing a lot of individual friendships that would detract from the relationship. I mean, I think it's important to honor your relationship and to make certain that you're giving time to that.

But with her work schedule so many years, working till eight o'clock at night and I always have been able to have dinner with friends and keep meeting people. It was always that I'd say: Honey, we need to have friends, we need to meet people. And that she's doing this. It's like she now has a best friend. I mean, she hasn't had a friend since the time I met her.

ELAINE: Since I was a teenager.

L: And it's wonderful because I see when they're together they're just like two little three-year-olds agitating each other.

E: And agitating everyone around us. . . . Oh, and the other big thing is that we found a church.

L: And it was neat, when I was really scared, to be able to call our priest and say: We really need you to pray for us on Sunday. This is really hard. They're all coming after us. We're really scared.

E: That was really new.

L: Because Elaine and I are both pretty spiritual people and we were both raised in a pretty rigid, structured religious tradition. I was raised as an Episcopalian and Elaine was raised as a Lutheran. And later converted to Episcopalianism. I mean, both of us had avoided the church for years simply because of the homophobia associated with it. Just not being willing to do that. And we found an Episcopal church that's a welcome, what they call a welcoming congregation and they actively seek out . . . lesbians to come to their congregation.

Because of their membership in that church, Elaine and Lisa were considering a commitment ceremony.

LISA: We've had up times and bad times, you know, up times and down times, but it's our lives and it's something that we're committed to working through, so it just seems like life.

ELAINE: And, I guess, too, the responses we've had from folks around here . . . we've gotten a real sense of how different we are.

L: People will tell us, straight people, that we're the healthiest couple they know. I don't know quite what to make of that, you know.

E: I think I just assumed that most couples were as connected as we are. Like with the psychic stuff, where I'm thinking and doing something and thinking it's me and it's actually that she's wanting to have happen and somehow I pick that up and I'm doing it. I just kind of thought couples do that.

L: I mean, we're just really into each other. It just gets more intense the longer we're together. We've both done so much individual therapy to work on our individual issues, so it just really enhances us as a couple. We communicate well, we're very authentic with each other. Neither of us is really afraid to share anything with the other. It may be uncomfortable but we don't have secrets from each other.

We all know that we all have thoughts and feelings that we're embarrassed about or that are shameful to us and yet, she and I will sit down and talk about these private experiences and be validated.

E: The thing with now having good friends is I now have a friend who is so much like me that when Lisa kind of tilts her head at something I'm going through, I can go to Leise and she goes: Oh yeah, and then starts talking. And you've got that with Sally and Louise. That support's been really important. We just can't do it all.

Later in the conversation, Elaine spoke of the depth of their relationship.

ELAINE: I think we both had a lot of therapy and resolved a lot of issues about things like vulnerability and we're much more vulnerable with each other and more powerful with each other.

It's like I'm more willing to speak up now and less afraid of her anger. I think part of the wisdom is that we've been together so long and we've had enough therapy that when we're going through something, we each know what's really our piece and we aren't projecting it onto the other.

LISA: And because we've watched how hard each of us has worked to resolve those issues, there's an incredible trust there and either one of us can be vulnerable and very, very open to each other.

Elaine and Lisa had a chance to think about the meaning of sharing their stories.

ELAINE: It's really nice to get back feedback that we've worked hard and it's working. It's like so much of the world discounts relationships between women whether they're friendships or intimate relationships. It's just really nice that we've been able to talk about and show what women can do together. My sense was people will take what we've done and take the pieces that work for them and leave the others behind.

And the reactions from other church members have fueled more thought from Lisa.

LISA: It happens every day and it's an interesting thing. They get to watch us, see how we function, how we treat each other, how we treat them, how we function in church, they see the value of our faith. I think you open people's hearts and minds to something that they never really had to think about.

ELAINE: It's like many of us have had to do this without any models and I thought about that a lot, especially as a sociologist, and all of a sudden they go "wow" and we're providing a model. I'm doing that. And that relationship that provides a model is built on deep and intense intimacy, emotional and physical.

E: Part of it was, I think we each had an intuitive sense about each other that we were both healthier than anybody we'd been with before. And that we wanted to see where it would go.

L: I think we're both romantics and idealists. I mean we both are intense people and we're very feeling people. It's what we've always wanted. I don't think either one of us ever wanted anything out of life but to love somebody fully and to be loved by somebody fully.

And I can remember the first time we were together and we got up the next morning . . . And she was the most gentle human being that morning. I mean, there was a softness about her, there was an availability. I had never felt so connected to a human being like that in my life. And at some gut, instinctive level, I thought to myself: This is the real thing. And I've got to do whatever I need to do to sustain this. It's as clear as if it happened yesterday.

Later, she picked up the thought about their relationship developing over time.

LISA: I think that when you're in your twenties and your thirties, you're struggling to make a living, you're struggling to figure out what you're going to do with your life. There's a quality to your energy that's different from when you are in your forties.

. . . I think that your relationship sort of goes with that. And I think from a developmental perspective, we've come to a very introspective part of our lives, and I mean, we're both bright people and we actually think about things. We now sort of watch life and witness life at a slower pace. We form opinions about that from our perspectives of people our age. We talk about that and it enriches us. I mean, you read things and they talk about mature love. You know, we've gotten there. And it's not that we don't still feel incredible passion for each other and energy for each other . . . there's just a grounded quality.

As for their physical relationship, they have gone through so much pain learning to recognize what has come from their pasts, and how to deal with it. But they have stuck with the work.

ELAINE: Making love is a very strong way of communicating who I am and what I feel about her, and so to not have that avenue was very painful. And I think because of how defended I've been too, it's like right after orgasm, that I can relax enough to let her in and really close and that's what you experienced that first morning.

LISA: And I come from the opposite perspective. The ultimate is emotional intimacy. I would die for you and that's the ultimate. You know, sex is how we use each other. That's how people use people . . . So, I mean, I don't put sex and love together, or didn't for a long time.

They continue to work on their relationship, and reap the benefits.

ELAINE: I think we've gotten more affectionate with each other.

LISA: Oh, I've always been affectionate.

E: But you're more relaxed now and I think it's trusting each other more sexually and so we can be physically closer without feeling threatened. I realize that I'm not as verbal as I thought I was, because she's very well into telling me how attractive I am or that she really missed me and it's like I may have all that stuff but I don't put it out there, so I'm working to say more. But we both thrive on touch.

L: And holding. I mean, we hold each other a lot.

As for their relationship now?

ELAINE: I said to Lisa it doesn't matter who I've talked to, it could be gay clients, lesbian clients, friends, when I've said that we're going to be together, retire together and do all that, they are always skeptical. And I say to them, this isn't just hope, this is a plan and the way we run our lives, we're working to ensure that.

Lisa's thoughts came into perspective for her during her campaign.

LISA: It was like: it was her and I and one of two things was going to happen. We were either not going to survive the process and have to completely change our lives and the direction of our lives, or we were going to survive the process. But either way it was OK with us.

I mean, it was just a fundamental realization that all of it really doesn't matter because we have each other. And that's the only thing that either one of us can't live without.

Bibliography

As we said before, no story comes from thin air. This work is based on a dissertation written by Dr. Lynn Haley-Banez.

Basseches, M., *Dialectical Thinking and Adult Development*. Norwood, NJ: Ablex Publishing Company, 1984.

Bell, S.E., Becoming a Political Woman: The Reconstruction and Interpretation of Experience Through Stories, in Alexandra D. Todd and Sue Fisher (eds.), *Gender and Discourse: The Power of Talk*. Norwood, NJ: Ablex Publishing Company, 1988.

Berzon, B., *Permanent Partners: Building Gay and Lesbian Relationships That Last*. New York: Penguin Books, 1988.

Blumstein, P. and Schwartz, P., *American Couples: Money, Work, Sex*. William Morrow and Company, 1983.

Bruner, J., *Acts of Meaning*. Cambridge, MA: Harvard University Press, 1990.

Bubenzer, D. and West, J., Interview with Kenneth J. Gergen: Social Construction, Families and Therapy, *The Family Journal: Counseling and Therapy for Couples and Families, 1*, 1993.

Burch, B., Another Perspective on Merger in Lesbian Relationships, in L. Rosewater and L. Walker (eds.), *Handbook of Feminist Therapy*. New York: Springer, 1985.

Campbell, S.M., *The Couple's Journey: Intimacy As a Path to Wholeness*. San Luis Obispo, CA: Impact Publishers, 1980.

Carr, D., *Time, Narrative and History*. Bloomington, IN: Indiana University Press, 1991.

Clunis D.M. and Green, G.D., *Lesbian Couples*. Seattle, WA: Seal Press, 1993.

De Cecco, J.P. and Elia, J.P., Critique and Synthesis of Biological Essentialism and Social Constructionist Views of Sexuality and Gender, *Journal of Homosexuality, 24*, 1993.

Decker, B., Counseling Gay and Lesbian Couples, *Journal of Social Work and Human Sexuality, 7*, 1984.

Deely, J., *The Human Use of Signs*. Lanham, MD: Rowman and Littlefield Publishers Inc., 1994.

Eco, U., *Six Walks in the Fictional Woods*. Cambridge, MA: Harvard University Press, 1994.

Epston D. and White, M., *Experience, Contradiction, Narrative and Imagination: Selected Papers of David Epston and Michael White, 1989-1991*. Adelaide, Australia: Dulwich Centre Publications, 1992.

Faderman, L., *Surpassing the Love of Men: Romantic Friendship and Love Between Two Women from the Renaissance to the Present*. New York: William Morrow and Company, 1981.

Falco, K.L., *Psychotherapy with Lesbian Clients: Theory into Practice*. New York: Bruner/Mazel, 1991.

Gergen, K., *The Saturated Self: Dilemmas of Identity in Contemporary Life*. New York: Basic Books, 1991.

Gergen, K., The Social Constructionist Movement in Modern Psychology, *American Psychologist, 40*, 1985.

Gergen, K.J. and Gergen, M.M., Narratives of the Self, in Theodore R. Sarbin and Karl E. Scheibe (eds.), *Studies in Social Identity*. New York: Praeger, 1983.

Gilligan, S. and Price, R., *Therapeutic Conversations*. New York: Norton, 1993.

Harry, J., Gay and Lesbian Relationships: Decade Review of the Literature, in E. Macklin and R.H. Rubin (eds.), *Contemporary Families and Alternative Lifestyles*. Beverly Hills, CA: Sage Publications, 1983.

Hutter, J.H., The Social Construction of Homosexuals in the Nineteenth Century: The Shift from the Sin to the Influence of Medicine on Criminalizing Sodomy in Germany, *Journal of Homosexuality, 24*, 1993.

Johnson, S.E., *Staying Power: Long-Term Lesbian Couples*. Tallahassee, FL: Naiad Press, 1994.

Jordan, J., Kaplan, A., Miller, J.B., Stiver, I., and Surrey, J., *Women's Growth in Connection—Writings from the Stone Center*. New York: Guilford Press, 1991.

Kaufman, P. Harrison, E., and Hyde, M., Distancing for Intimacy in Lesbian Relationships, *American Journal of Psychiatry, 141*, 1984.

Kitzinger, C., *The Social Construction of Lesbianism*. London, UK: Sage Publications, 1987.

Kitzinger, C. and Wilkinson, S., Transitions from Heterosexuality to Lesbianism: The Discursive Production of Lesbian Identities, *Developmental Psychology, 31*, 1995.

Lather, P., Feminist Perspectives on Empowering Research Methodologies, *Women's Studies International Forum, 11,* 1988.

Lindebaum, J.P., The Shattering of an Illusion: The Problem of Competition in Lesbian Relationships, *Feminist Studies, 11,* 1985.

McAdams, D.P., *The Stories We Live By: Personal Myths and the Making of Self.* New York: William Morrow and Company, 1993.

McDaniel, J., *The Lesbian Couples' Guide.* New York: HarperPerennial, 1995.

McWhirter, D.P. and Mattison, A.M., *The Male Couple: How Relationships Develop.* Englewood Cliffs, NJ: Prentice-Hall, 1984.

Mencher, J., Intimacy in Lesbian Relationships: A Critical Re-Examination of Fusion, Work in Progress, No. 42. Wellesley, MA: Stone Center Working Paper Series, 1990.

Mishler, E.G., The Analysis of Interview-Narratives, in Theodore R. Sabin (ed.), *Narrative Psychology.* New York: Praeger, 1986.

Oakley, A., Interviewing Women: A Contradiction in Terms, in H. Roberts (ed.), *Doing Feminist Research.* London, UK: Routledge and Kegan Paul, 1981.

Peplau, L.A., Research on Homosexual Couples: An Overview, *Journal of Homosexuality, 8,* 1982.

Peplau, L.A., Padesky, C., and Hamilton, M., Loving Women: Attachment and Autonomy in Lesbian Relationships, *Journal of Social Issues, 34,* 1978.

Pharr, S., *Homophobia: A Weapon of Sexism.* Little Rock, AK: Chardon Press, 1988.

Phelan, S., (Be)Coming Out: Lesbian Identity and Politics, *Signs: Journal of Women in Culture and Society, 18,* 1993.

Ponse, B., *Identities in the Lesbian World: The Social Construction of Self.* Westport, CT: Greenwood, 1978.

Rich, A., Women and Honor: Some Notes on Lying, in Adrienne Rich (ed.), *On Lies, Secrets and Silence.* New York: W.W. Norton and Company, 1979.

Ricouer, P., *Time and Narrative.* Chicago: University of Chicago Press, 1984.

Riessman, C.K., *Divorce Talk: Women and Men Make Sense of Personal Relationships.* New Brunswick, NJ: Rutgers University Press, 1990.

Robson, R., *Cecile.* Ithaca, NY: Firebrand Books, 1991.

Rust, P.A., Coming Out in the Age of Social Constructionism: Sexual Identity Formation Among Lesbians and Bisexual Women, *Gender and Society, 7,* 1993.

Sang, B., New Directions in Lesbian Research, Theory and Education, *Journal of Counseling and Development, 68,* 1989.

Shotter, J. and Gergen, K., *Texts of Identity.* London, UK: Sage Publications, 1989.

Tanner, D.M., *The Lesbian Couple.* Lexington, MA: Lexington Books, 1978.

Vetere, V.A., The Role of Friendship in the Development and Maintenance of Lesbian Love Relationships, *Journal of Homosexuality, 8,* 1982.

Webster's Seventh New Collegiate Dictionary, p. 592. Springfield, MA: G. & C. Merriam Company, Publishers, 1971.

White, M. and Epston, D., *Narrative Means to Therapeutic Ends.* New York: Norton, 1990.

About the Authors

Lynn Haley-Banez, PhD, is an assistant professor in the Counselor Education Department at Fairfield University in Connecticut. Dr. Haley-Banez is also a consultant/trainer for working with diverse and LGBT populations in clinical settings. She has recently written and produced training videos and texts for working with LGBT students and families, and has presented professional workshops on the topic of lesbian couples at national and international conferences.

Joanne Garrett has been a journalist for twenty-five years and has been recognized for investigative reporting and headline writing. She is a copy editor at a publication in Seattle, Washington, as well as a freelance editor and writer.

Order a copy of this book with this form or online at:
http://www.haworthpressinc.com/store/product.asp?sku=4678

LESBIANS IN COMMITTED RELATIONSHIPS
Extraordinary Couples, Ordinary Lives

_____in hardbound at $34.95 (ISBN: 1-56023-208-0)

_____in softbound at $17.95 (ISBN: 1-56023-209-9)

COST OF BOOKS_____

OUTSIDE USA/CANADA/
MEXICO: ADD 20%____

POSTAGE & HANDLING_____
(US: $4.00 for first book & $1.50
for each additional book)
Outside US: $5.00 for first book
& $2.00 for each additional book)

SUBTOTAL_____

in Canada: add 7% GST____

STATE TAX____
(NY, OH & MIN residents, please
add appropriate local sales tax)

FINAL TOTAL____
(If paying in Canadian funds,
convert using the current
exchange rate, UNESCO
coupons welcome.)

☐ **BILL ME LATER:** ($5 service charge will be added)
(Bill-me option is good on US/Canada/Mexico orders only;
not good to jobbers, wholesalers, or subscription agencies.)

☐ Check here if billing address is different from
shipping address and attach purchase order and
billing address information.

Signature_____

☐ **PAYMENT ENCLOSED: $_____**

☐ **PLEASE CHARGE TO MY CREDIT CARD.**

☐ Visa ☐ MasterCard ☐ AmEx ☐ Discover
☐ Diner's Club ☐ Eurocard ☐ JCB

Account # _____

Exp. Date_____

Signature_____

Prices in US dollars and subject to change without notice.

NAME_____
INSTITUTION_____
ADDRESS_____
CITY_____
STATE/ZIP_____
COUNTRY_____ COUNTY (NY residents only)_____
TEL_____ FAX_____
E-MAIL_____
May we use your e-mail address for confirmations and other types of information? ☐ Yes ☐ No
We appreciate receiving your e-mail address and fax number. Haworth would like to e-mail or fax special
discount offers to you, as a preferred customer. **We will never share, rent, or exchange your e-mail address
or fax number.** We regard such actions as an invasion of your privacy.

Order From Your Local Bookstore or Directly From
The Haworth Press, Inc.
10 Alice Street, Binghamton, New York 13904-1580 • USA
TELEPHONE: 1-800-HAWORTH (1-800-429-6784) / Outside US/Canada: (607) 722-5857
FAX: 1-800-895-0582 / Outside US/Canada: (607) 722-6362
E-mail: getinfo@haworthpressinc.com
PLEASE PHOTOCOPY THIS FORM FOR YOUR PERSONAL USE.
www.HaworthPress.com

BOF02